CONTROL THE BRAND

How to Build, Protect, and Scale a Business That Dominates Its Market

Ruben Alcoba

For my daughter,
Juliet Alcoba, Esq.

An exceptional trademark attorney
and the future of our firm.

May this book serve as a tool
to guide your clients,
protect what they build,
and help them understand the value
of what you help them create.

This is part of your legacy now.

Disclaimer

This book is provided for informational and educational purposes only and does not constitute legal advice. Reading this book does not create an attorney-client relationship between the reader and the author or any affiliated law firm, including Alcoba Law Group PA.

Trademark law, intellectual property strategy, and business structuring involve fact-specific considerations. Readers are strongly encouraged to consult qualified legal counsel regarding their specific circumstances before making any decisions based on the information contained herein.

No Guarantees

While every effort has been made to ensure the accuracy of the information presented, the author makes no representations or warranties, express or implied, regarding the completeness, accuracy, or applicability of the content. The author shall not be liable for any damages or losses arising from the use or reliance upon this material.

Business and Strategy Disclaimer

Any references to business strategies, market positioning, valuation considerations, or growth frameworks are general in nature and may not apply to all businesses or industries. Outcomes vary based on execution, market conditions, and individual circumstances.

Third-Party References and Acknowledgment

This book references publicly known historical figures, business leaders, and widely cited strategic works for educational and illustrative purposes.

All references to individuals such as Sun Tzu, Steve Jobs, Phil Knight, Bernard Arnault, and Adolphus Busch are based on publicly available information and are used solely for commentary, analysis, and educational discussion.

No affiliation, endorsement, or sponsorship by any referenced individual, estate, company, or organization is implied.

Fair Use Notice

Certain quotations, principles, and references, particularly those attributed to historical works such as *The Art of War*, are believed to be in the public domain or are used in accordance with fair use principles for purposes of commentary, criticism, and education.

Trademark Notice

All trademarks, service marks, trade names, and logos referenced in this book are the property of their respective owners. Their use is for identification and educational purposes only and does not imply endorsement.

Professional Responsibility Statement

This book reflects the professional experience and opinions of the author as a trademark and intellectual property attorney. It is not intended to replace individualized legal analysis or professional judgment.

Contact Information

For inquiries regarding permissions, licensing, or legal services:

Alcoba Law Group PA
7791 NW 46 Street, Suite 218
Doral, Florida 33166
Tel: 305-362-8118
Email: alcoba@alcobalaw.com
Website: www.alcobalaw.com

Final Notice

The strategies discussed in this book are designed to help readers think more strategically about trademarks, branding, and business structure. Implementation of any strategy should be done carefully, with professional guidance where appropriate.

First Edition

Table of Contents

Contents

PROLOGUE

Most business owners do not think about trademarks strategically.

They think about them when something feels at risk.

When a name begins to matter.
When a competitor appears too close.
When a platform refuses to act.
When a deal begins to take shape and someone asks a simple question:

"Do you own the brand?"

By that point, the position is already being tested.

And in many cases, it is already too late to control it cleanly.

For years, I have represented founders, operators, and companies at every stage of growth.

Some were just beginning, trying to secure a name before entering the market.

Others were scaling, navigating distribution, partnerships, and expansion across channels.

And some were at the most critical moment of all:

Being evaluated.

By investors.
By partners.
By buyers.

Across all these situations, one pattern appears consistently.

The companies that win are not the ones that file trademarks.

They are the ones that understand what the trademark does.

Most businesses treat trademarks as protection.

A defensive tool.

Something to prevent others from taking what they have built.

That understanding is incomplete.

And in many cases, it is the reason control is lost.

A trademark is not just a legal right.

It is a system.

A system that determines how your brand is used,
who is allowed to participate in it,
how your product is priced,
how your business expands,
and how your company is valued.

When that system is understood and applied correctly, something changes.

You stop reacting to the market.

You begin shaping it.

Competitors hesitate.
Distribution follows structure.
Pricing stabilizes.
Growth becomes controlled.

When it is not understood, the opposite occurs.

The brand spreads, but its meaning weakens.
Access increases, but control disappears.
Revenue grows, but value becomes uncertain.

And eventually, the business is forced to compete on terms it never intended to accept.

This book was not written as a legal guide.

It was written to change how you think about the role of a trademark in your business.

Each chapter addresses a specific point where companies gain or lose control.

Not in theory.

In practice.

Through decisions that appear small at the time but define the outcome over the long term.

If you approach this book as a checklist, you will miss its purpose.

If you approach it as a system, you will begin to see how each part connects.

Because in the end, the question is not whether you have a trademark.

The question is whether you control everything that flows through it.

INTRODUCTION

Most business books are read for information.
This one is not.

It is read for position.

Because the difference between businesses that grow and businesses that control their market is not effort. It is not timing. It is not even product.

It is structure.

And at the center of that structure is something most companies misunderstand from the beginning.

The trademark.

Not as a filing.
Not as a legal requirement.
Not as protection.

As a system.

A system that determines who is allowed to participate in your business, how your brand is perceived, how your product is priced, how your company expands, and how it is ultimately valued when someone else evaluates it.

Most business owners encounter trademarks reactively.

When a name becomes important.
When a competitor appears too close.
When a platform fails to respond.
When a deal begins to take shape and someone asks a question that should have been answered much earlier:

"Do you own the brand?"

By that point, the business has already formed around assumptions.

Assumptions about ownership.
Assumptions about control.
Assumptions about how the brand can be used, expanded, and protected.

Some of those assumptions are correct.

Many are not.

And when they are not, the consequences do not appear immediately.

They appear later.

When distribution becomes inconsistent.
When pricing begins to erode.
When competitors enter more easily than expected.
When partnerships become difficult to structure.
When investors hesitate.
When buyers begin to ask questions that cannot be answered clearly.

This book exists to change that outcome.

It is not designed to teach trademark law in the traditional sense. It is not a procedural guide, and it is not a checklist of filings.

It is a framework.

Each chapter isolates a point where businesses gain or lose control. Not in theory, but in practice. Through decisions that appear small at the time, but compound into structural advantages or structural weaknesses.

The goal is not to overwhelm you with doctrine.

The goal is to shift how you think.

Because once you understand how a trademark functions as a system, you begin to see connections that were not visible before.

You begin to recognize that:

Distribution is not separate from branding.
Pricing is not separate from perception.
Expansion is not separate from control.
And value is not separate from structure.

They are all connected.

And the trademark sits at the center of that connection.

There is a pattern that appears across industries, markets, and company sizes.

Businesses that treat trademarks as protection operate defensively. They respond to problems as they arise. They react to competitors. They attempt to correct issues after they have already formed.

Businesses that treat trademarks as systems operate differently.

They define conditions before entering markets.
They control how their brand moves through distribution.
They shape perception before comparison occurs.
And they position themselves in a way that reduces the need for constant enforcement.

They do not eliminate competition.

They change how competition occurs.

That shift is not theoretical.

It is structural.

And it is available to any business that understands how to apply it.

This book is written to give you that perspective.

Not so that you can file better.

So that you can build differently.

Because once you understand what a trademark does, the question is no longer whether you have one.

The question becomes:

What does it allow you to control?

And once you begin to answer that question clearly, the way you build your business will not remain the same.

By the end of this book, you will not just understand trademarks differently.

You will understand how to:

- structure your brand for control from the beginning
- prevent competitors from entering your position
- scale without losing pricing power or consistency
- and build an asset that increases in value as your business grows

This is not about filing better.

It is about building something that cannot be easily replaced.

Before You Begin

This is not a book to read once.

It is a system to revisit as your business evolves.

Each chapter addresses a point where companies gain or lose control. Some will apply immediately. Others will become relevant as you scale.

Do not try to apply everything at once.

Instead, read with one question in mind:

"Where am I currently losing control?"

Start there.

Then build forward.

Part I: Foundations of Control

Chapter 1

Why Trademarks Control Markets (Not Just Protect Them)

The Founder believed he had finally secured the brand.

After a year of steady growth, the name had started to carry weight. Customers recognized it. Distributors were beginning to ask for it specifically. It felt like something was forming, something that could scale.

So, he did what most founders eventually do.

He filed the trademark.

The process was straightforward. The application was prepared, submitted, and a few months later, approved. The registration came through cleanly, covering the core product category. He updated his packaging, added the ® symbol, and made sure the brand appeared consistently across his website and sales channels.

It was a clear step forward.

More importantly, it felt like closure.

The concern that someone could take the name, or build around it, seemed resolved. With that behind him, he turned his attention back to growth.

He expanded distribution.
He opened new channels.
He focused on volume.

And for a time, the decision appeared to have done exactly what he intended.

Strategic Principle

> *"All warfare is based on deception."* Sun Tzu

Control perception and you influence every decision that follows.

Most companies believe a trademark is something you file after you build a business.

That belief is not just incomplete, it is dangerous.

Because the companies that consistently win in competitive markets understand something much earlier. They understand that a trademark is not a legal formality. It is not a document, and it is not a defensive mechanism waiting to be used.

It is a system.

And once you begin to see it that way, everything changes.

A trademark, at its most basic level, tells a customer who they are buying from. That seems simple. Almost administrative. But in business, simple functions often carry disproportionate power.

Once a name becomes associated with quality, consistency, and trust, the transaction changes. The customer is no longer comparing products. The customer is buying certainty.

And certainty is what people pay for.

Most business owners never move beyond what can be called protection thinking. They believe the purpose of a trademark is to prevent others from taking their name. They file, they receive a registration, and they move on.

But protection is only the beginning.

Control is where the strategy lives.

Control asks different questions. It asks who is allowed to sell under the brand. It asks where the product can appear and how it must be presented. It asks what expectations are attached to the name and whether competitors can enter the same space without creating confusion.

Those questions do not arise from legal theory. They arise from market behavior.

There is a principle in strategy that appears in many forms but always leads to the same conclusion: the strongest position is the one that does not need to be defended. When a brand is clearly defined, consistently presented, properly structured, and actively managed, something subtle begins to happen.

Competitors hesitate.

Platforms respond more quickly.

Distributors follow direction more closely.

The conflict never fully materializes, because the conditions that would create it have already been shaped.

This is what it means to control the market without appearing to fight for it.

The Founder, at this stage, had done what most would consider correct. He had secured the registration. He had aligned his materials. He had moved forward with confidence. But the effect of a trademark is not determined at the moment it is filed. It is determined by how it is used to shape everything that comes after.

And that is where most businesses begin to lose control.

Consider the difference between two companies selling nearly identical products. One struggles to maintain pricing. The other commands a premium without constant justification. The materials are similar. The manufacturing process is comparable. The difference lies in what surrounds the product.

The brand.

When a trademark carries meaning, it reduces comparison. When comparison is reduced, pricing becomes less sensitive. When pricing becomes less sensitive, margins stabilize. And when margins stabilize, the business gains room to expand without pressure.

This is not marketing theory. It is structural advantage.

The same principle applies to distribution. Many businesses, especially in early growth, expand access without restriction. They sell to anyone willing to buy. They pursue visibility without considering control. For a time, this accelerates growth.

Then something shifts.

Pricing becomes inconsistent. The brand appears differently across channels. Unauthorized sellers begin to surface. Competitors enter with similar positioning. What once felt like expansion begins to resemble fragmentation.

The issue is not distribution itself. It is the absence of structure behind it.

A trademark, when used correctly, allows a company to define the terms under which its brand can move. It does not require ownership of every channel. It requires influence over how the brand is used within those channels.

That distinction determines whether the company controls the market or takes part in it.

The same dynamic extends into expansion. A strong brand reduces friction. It allows entry into new markets without starting from zero. It creates opportunities for partnerships, licensing, and scale that would otherwise require significant capital and infrastructure.

But expansion without control produces the same outcome as distribution without control. The brand spreads, but its meaning weakens.

And when meaning weakens, value follows.

Busch Today: What He Would Do (And What the Law Limits)

Adolphus Busch built his business in a way that, at the time, seemed aggressive but logical.

He did not simply produce beer and rely on others to distribute it.

He built a system around it.

He invested in how the product moved, where it appeared, and who controlled access to it. He understood, long before the language existed, that the brand was not just something customers recognized, it was something that could shape the entire market around it.

If Busch were building that same business today, his instinct would not change.

He would not stop at protecting the name.

He would use the trademark to decide who is allowed inside the system, how the product is presented, and what level of consistency must be maintained for the brand to retain its meaning.

He would build agreements around that control. He would restrict access where necessary. He would remove those who operated outside the structure.

But the modern environment imposes limits that did not exist in his time.

Distribution systems are regulated. Competition law places boundaries on how far control can extend. Certain forms of price and territorial restriction are examined closely. The ability to dominate every layer of the system is no longer absolute.

That is where modern strategy exists.

Not in trying to control everything without limitation, but in understanding how far control can extend before it becomes a liability.

A trademark, then, is not a filing.

It is not an isolated act.

It is a structure that connects ownership, consistency, control, and enforcement into a system that determines how the business works in the market.

When these elements are aligned, the brand becomes more than a name. It becomes an asset that carries value forward, across products, across markets, and ultimately into the moment where the business is evaluated by someone else.

At that point, the question is no longer whether the company generates revenue. The question is whether the brand itself can be trusted to continue generating it under new ownership.

That is where the real value appears.

Most companies do not fail because they lack growth. They fail because they do not control what they have built as it grows.

The Founder, like many others, believed that securing the trademark had resolved the issue. In reality, it had only defined the starting point.

What followed would determine whether the brand became something that could be defended, or something that could be directed.

Closing Observation

At the time, nothing appeared wrong.
That was the problem.

Chapter 2

Amazon Brand Registry: Why Most Sellers Get It Wrong (And How to Fix It)

The Founder saw it as the last step.

The product was selling. Reviews were coming in. The listing had traction, and for the first time, it felt like the business was no longer fragile. There was momentum behind it.

But with that momentum came something else.

Other sellers.

At first, it was subtle. A new seller appeared on the listing. Then another. Prices began to move slightly. Nothing dramatic, but enough to notice.

So, he did what most founders are told to do.

He registered the trademark.
He enrolled in Amazon Brand Registry.

The process felt official. Structured. Legitimate.

Once approved, he believed the problem had been solved.

Now, he thought, Amazon would step in.

Now, the system would protect him.

He filed his first complaint.

Then another.

And another.

Some were removed. Others were rejected. A few disappeared, only to reappear later under different names, slightly modified listings, or new sellers entirely.

The pattern was not consistent.

The results were not predictable.

And the control he expected never fully materialized.

Still, from the outside, it looked like he had done everything correctly.

Strategic Principle

> *"He who is skilled in attack flashes forth from the topmost heights of heaven."* Sun Tzu

Precision wins faster than force. Clarity wins faster than effort.

Most sellers believe Amazon Brand Registry is protection.

It is not.

It is a tool.

And like any tool, its effectiveness depends entirely on how it is used.

Thousands of brands are enrolled in Brand Registry at any given time. Many of them still lose control of their listings, their pricing, and ultimately their reputation. The problem is not the system itself.

The problem is how the system is understood.

Amazon does not function like a court. It does not create rights, and it does not guarantee enforcement. It reacts.

It reacts to clarity.

It reacts to consistency.

And most importantly, it reacts to evidence.

This distinction is where most sellers begin to lose control.

A trademark creates legal rights. That is the foundation. Brand Registry sits on top of that foundation as an operational layer: a way to assert those rights within Amazon's ecosystem.

If the underlying trademark is weak, inconsistent, or unclear, Brand Registry reflects that weakness. If the trademark is strong and consistently applied, Brand Registry becomes significantly more effective.

But the system itself does not compensate for poor strategy.

It exposes it.

Most sellers enter Brand Registry with a simple expectation: that once enrolled, Amazon will protect their brand. That assumption creates a false sense of security, and from that point forward, every decision begins to drift in the wrong direction.

Amazon does not respond to frustration. It is not evaluating fairness. It is not weighing who deserves to win.

It is evaluating whether the claim presented is clear, specific, and supported by evidence tied to an enforceable right.

When a complaint is submitted, the system asks a small set of questions. Does the party submitting the complaint own the trademark? Is the mark used in a way that creates confusion? Is there a clear misuse tied to that mark?

If the answers are uncertain, the complaint fails.

Not because the claim is wrong, but because it is unclear.

This is where the difference between effort and precision becomes visible.

Many sellers respond to perceived infringement with volume. They submit multiple complaints. They escalate emotionally. They attempt to remove sellers who are affecting their pricing or their position.

But not every problem on Amazon is a trademark problem.

This is one of the most important distinctions in this entire system.

A counterfeit product is a trademark issue. A product that misuses the brand name is a trademark issue. But a seller offering a genuine product at a lower price is not.

Attempting to use trademark enforcement to solve distribution problems rarely works. And when it fails repeatedly, it begins to reduce credibility within the system.

Amazon is not evaluating whether a seller should be there. It is evaluating whether the trademark has been violated.

That difference determines everything.

The deeper issue, however, often begins before Amazon is even involved.

Weak trademarks create weak enforcement. Descriptive names blur boundaries. Inconsistent use across packaging, listings, and branding creates confusion not only for customers, but for the enforcement system itself.

When a brand appears under multiple variations, slight changes by competitors become harder to distinguish from legitimate use. The line between infringement and variation becomes less clear.

And when the line is unclear, enforcement slows down.

This is why consistency becomes a strategic advantage. Not because it looks professional, but because it defines the boundaries of the brand in a way that can be recognized and enforced.

Amazon, at its core, is a pattern-recognition system.

It responds to structured inputs.

When the brand is clearly defined, consistently used, and supported by evidence, enforcement becomes faster and more predictable. When those elements are missing, the system hesitates.

And hesitation, in a competitive marketplace, is enough to lose control.

There is also a tendency among sellers to treat Brand Registry as a completed task. They enroll, upload their assets, and move on. Meanwhile, the marketplace continues to change.

New sellers enter. Listings evolve. Variations appear.

Without active monitoring, the system interprets inaction as acceptance. Over time, unauthorized behavior becomes normalized, not because it is correct, but because it is unchallenged.

Control, in this environment, is not passive.

It requires observation.

It requires selective action.

Discipline is essential.

There is a final risk that is less obvious, but equally important.

Overuse of the system.

Some sellers, frustrated by lack of control, begin to file complaints aggressively. They attempt to remove anything that affects their position. They expand the definition of infringement beyond what the system recognizes.

And slowly, something changes.

Their complaints carry less weight.
Their requests move more slowly.
Their credibility begins to erode.

Amazon does not announce this shift. But it occurs.

Precision is replaced by noise.

Unwanted noise is eliminated.

The strategy, then, is not to act more, but to act better.

To focus on clear violations. To build evidence before acting. To maintain consistency in how the brand is presented and defended.

Amazon is not a battlefield.

It is an environment where the strategy is tested.

Real control is established before the product ever reaches the platform, through the strength of the trademark, the clarity of the brand, and the structure behind how it is distributed.

When those elements align, Brand Registry becomes a powerful extension of that system.

When they are not, it becomes a reflection of the underlying weaknesses.

Closing Observation

It was not the system that failed him.
It was what he expected the system to do.

Chapter 3

How Companies Lose Their Trademark Without Knowing It

The Founder never decided to give anything up.

If anything, he believed he was protecting what he had built.

The brand had grown. The product line expanded. New opportunities began to appear—partnerships, distributors, even early licensing discussions. Each one felt like progress. Each one felt like a natural next step.

He allowed a distributor to adjust packaging slightly for a new market.
He approved a partner's use of the brand in a format that "worked better" for their channel.
He let a reseller change product descriptions to improve conversion.

None of it felt significant.

Each decision solved a slight problem. Each one made the business move a little faster.

And because nothing broke at once, there was no reason to question the pattern.

Customers were still buying.
Revenue was still growing.
The brand was still visible.

From the outside, everything appeared intact.

Over time, however, something began to shift.

The brand started to appear in slightly different forms. The presentation varied depending on where it was seen. Some versions felt stronger than others. Some felt less controlled.

But there was no single moment where it was clear something had gone wrong.

Only a gradual change.

And by the time it became noticeable, it was difficult to trace back to any one decision.

Strategic Principle

"If you know the enemy and know yourself, you need not fear the result of a hundred battles." Sun Tzu

The greatest risks are rarely external. They form inside the system you believe you control.

Most business owners believe trademarks are lost in court.

They imagine a lawsuit, a direct challenge, a moment where something is taken from them.

That is not how it usually happens.

Trademarks are not lost in a single event. They are lost gradually, through decisions that appear reasonable at the time, repeated without recognizing their cumulative effect.

There is no warning.
No clear turning point.
No moment that signals the shift.

Only a slow weakening of control.

This is one of the most dangerous realities in trademark strategy: a company can lose the strength of its trademark without anyone ever trying to take it.

Because the greatest risk is not external.

It is internal.

A trademark is not kept by registration alone. It depends on a small set of conditions that must remain intact over time. It must be used. It must be used consistently. And it must be controlled.

When any of these begin to break down, the trademark does not disappear at once. It simply becomes less defined.

And when a brand becomes less defined, it becomes easier to challenge, easier to copy, and harder to enforce.

The first way this happens is through inactivity.

When a company stops using its trademark in commerce, even temporarily, it begins to create doubt about whether the brand is still active. Over time, that doubt becomes a presumption. And once that presumption forms, others can begin to occupy the space that was left unguarded.

This is not a dramatic process. It is quiet. A product line is paused. A business slows down. A return is planned for later. But while the company waits, the market does not.

Someone else moves in.

And when the original owner tries to return, the position is no longer as strong as it once was.

The second way control is lost is more subtle, and far more common.

It occurs when a company allows others to use its trademark without keeping oversight. At first, this feels like growth. More people using the brand means more exposure. More exposure suggests expansion.

But without control, exposure leads to inconsistency.

Products begin to vary in quality. Presentation shifts from one channel to another. The meaning attached to the brand begins to change, not intentionally, but inevitably.

And when a trademark no longer stands for a consistent level of quality or experience, it begins to lose its function.

In plain terms, if the brand no longer means something specific, it no longer belongs to anyone in a meaningful way.

The law reflects this reality.

Control is not optional in a trademark system. It is needed.

The third way a trademark weakens is through language itself.

When a brand becomes too successful, there is a tendency for customers to use it as shorthand for an entire category. The name stops identifying a source and begins identifying a type of product.

At first, this feels like dominance.

Then it becomes dilution.

Once the brand is no longer seen as distinct, exclusivity disappears. And without exclusivity, enforcement becomes increasingly difficult.

This is how well-known names have historically lost protection, not because they failed, but because they became too widely and loosely used.

Each of these paths, non-use, loss of control, and generic use, work quietly. None of them require a competitor to act aggressively. None of them depend on a legal dispute.

They depend only on the absence of discipline.

There are also less visible ways this weakening occurs.

Inconsistent branding is one of them. When a company uses multiple variations of its name, changes presentation often, or allows different versions to exist across products and channels, it reduces recognition. Over time, it becomes harder to define what the brand actually is.

Ownership structure is another. When the trademark is held by the wrong entity, or when assignments are unclear, control becomes fragmented. Even if the business appears stable, the underlying asset may not be.

Failure to enforce is often misunderstood. A company does not lose its trademark simply by choosing not to pursue every instance of misuse. But repeated tolerance of confusion, combined with widespread inconsistent use, gradually weakens the position.

None of these issues are visible at the beginning.

They do not stop growth.
They do not reduce revenue at once.
They do not trigger alarms.

Which is precisely why they are dangerous.

The consequences appear later.

Competitors begin to enter more easily. The brand becomes harder to distinguish. Pricing pressure increases as comparison becomes more direct. Expansion into new markets meets resistance, either from existing users or from a lack of clear ownership boundaries.

And when the business reaches a point where it is evaluated, by a partner, an investor, or a potential buyer, the weakness becomes visible.

At that point, it is no longer theoretical.

The brand, which once appeared to be an asset, is now a question.

Most businesses assume that once a trademark is secured, it stays secure.

Strategic businesses understand something different.

A trademark is not something you obtain.

It is something you maintain.

And maintenance is not passive.

It is a continuous act of control.

Closing Observation

Nothing was taken from him.
He simply stopped holding it together.

Chapter 4

If You Do Not Own the Brand, You Do Not Own the Business

Most founders believe they own their business.

They built it.
They funded it.
They run it every day.

From their perspective, ownership feels obvious.

But ownership, in business, is not determined by effort.

It is determined by control.

And in many companies, the most important asset, the one that determines recognition, trust, pricing, and long-term value, is not controlled the way the founder believes it is.

That asset is the brand.

And legally, the brand exists in one place.

The trademark.

Strategic Principle

"The general who holds the advantage holds the outcome." Sun Tzu

Control the critical asset, and you control the result, regardless of how the work was done.

Every business has assets.

Products. Inventory. Equipment. Contracts. Relationships.

But none of those assets determine how the market sees the business.

The brand does.

It determines whether customers recognize you, whether they trust you, and whether they are willing to pay a premium rather than compare alternatives.

It is the point of connection between the company and the market.

And unlike most assets, it is not spread across multiple systems.

It is anchored in a single legal structure.

The trademark.

This is where most businesses begin to misunderstand their own position.

They assume that because they use a name, they own that name. Because the brand appears on their product, their website, and their marketing, it must belong to them.

But use and ownership are not always aligned.

And when they are not, the consequences do not appear at once.

They appear at the worst possible moment.

Ownership, in the context of trademarks, is not informal.

It is defined by how the mark is used, how it is documented, and how it is structured across the entities involved in the business.

If that structure is unclear, control becomes uncertain.

And when control becomes uncertain, leverage disappears.

This is not a theoretical risk.

It is one of the most common reasons transactions slow down, partnerships collapse, and companies lose negotiating power when it matters most.

The problem is not that the business lacks value.

The problem is that the ownership of that value is not clear.

The pattern appears in different forms, but the result is always the same.

In some cases, the founder files the trademark personally, while the business operates through a separate entity. The brand is used by the company but legally held by the individual. At first, this seems harmless.

Until the business grows.

Until investors ask questions.

Until a buyer begins due diligence.

At that point, separation becomes a problem.

The entity generating revenue does not clearly control the asset driving that revenue.

And uncertainty enters the discussion.

In other cases, the brand evolves over time. Designers contribute. Partners participate. New variations are introduced. But the ownership of those contributions is never formally documented.

Everything works, until clarity is required.

And when clarity is required, it does not exist.

There are situations where companies allow others to use the brand, partners, affiliates, distributors, without defining how that use is controlled. The intention is expansion. The result is dilution.

Because when multiple parties begin to operate under the same name without structure, the distinction between ownership and access begins to fade.

And once that distinction fades, the brand weakens.

There are also businesses that try to create more advanced structures, placing trademarks in one entity and operations in another, but doing so without a clear plan. What was meant to create efficiency ends up creating confusion.

The issue is not complexity.

The issue is lack of design.

There is a principle in strategy that applies directly here.

Control the asset, and you control the outcome.

In most businesses, the asset that determines outcome is not the product.

It is the brand attached to it.

This becomes most visible when the business is evaluated by someone outside of it.

A buyer does not begin by asking how hard the founder worked. An investor does not begin by asking how much effort has gone into building the company.

They ask simpler, more direct questions.

Who owns the trademark?
Is that ownership clear?
Can it be transferred without complication?
Can it be scaled across markets?
Are there risks attached to it?

If the answers are uncertain, the response is predictable.

The value of the business decreases.

Not because the business is weak, but because the asset controlling the business is unclear.

If ownership is strong, documented, and aligned with the structure of the company, the opposite occurs.

Confidence increases.

And with it, value.

The correct way to think about trademarks is not as a filing.

It is a system that must be designed.

Ownership must be intentional. One entity must clearly hold the rights. That ownership must be documented in a way that leaves no ambiguity.

Use must be controlled. The brand must appear consistently, and any party using it must do so under defined conditions.

Structure must align with strategy. In more advanced businesses, this may involve separating the trademark into its own entity and licensing it to the operating company. But when this is done, it must be done with precision.

Because structure, without clarity, creates the same problem it was meant to solve.

And finally, ownership must align with where the business is going.

Growth, licensing, expansion, and eventual exit all depend on the strength and clarity of this single asset.

If that alignment does not exist, the limitations will appear later.

And later is when they are hardest to fix.

Most ownership problems stay invisible during growth.

Revenue increases. Operations expand. The business appears stable.

But ownership is not tested during growth.

It is tested during transition.

When a partner enters.
When capital is raised.
When the company is sold.

That is when structure becomes visible.

And that is when mistakes become expensive.

Most founders believe:

"We built the brand, so we own it."

Strategic operators think differently.

They understand that building and owning are not the same.

And that ownership must be structured in a way that cannot be questioned.

Closing Observation

He believed it was his because he built it.
The structure never confirmed it.

Chapter 5

How Nike, Apple, and Coca-Cola Use Trademarks to Dominate Markets

Most companies believe branding is a function of marketing.

They think in terms of logos, colors, campaigns, and visibility. They invest in attention, hoping that recognition will translate into growth.

But the companies that consistently dominate markets are not thinking about branding at that level.

They are thinking about control.

Not control in the sense of ownership alone, but control over how their brand is perceived, where it appears, how it is priced, and how it expands.

And once that control is established, competition changes.

Strategic Principle

> *"The supreme art of war is to subdue the enemy without fighting."* Sun Tzu

The strongest position is the one competitors hesitate to challenge.

Nike, Apple, and Coca-Cola do not compete the way most businesses do.

They do not rely on constant comparison. They do not depend on being the lowest price or the most accessible option. They operate from a position that has already been defined before the customer begins to evaluate alternatives.

They control perception first.

Everything else follows.

Nike does not begin with the product.

It begins with identity.

The Swoosh is not a description of a shoe. It does not explain materials, construction, or performance specifications. It represents something else entirely: discipline, performance, aspiration. When a customer sees it, the question is not whether the product is good.

That assumption has already been made.

And once that assumption is in place, comparison becomes secondary.

Apple operates in a similar way, but with a different form of control.

Its products are not introduced as technical solutions. They are presented as experiences: simple, refined, and complete. The brand signals that the product will function without friction, that it will integrate seamlessly into the user's life, and that it carries a certain level of status.

Again, the evaluation happens before the comparison.

Coca-Cola takes a different path but reaches the same result.

It does not rely on product differentiation. It relies on familiarity, consistency, and emotion. The brand is tied to memory, repetition, and expectation. The product becomes secondary to what it represents.

Across all three, the pattern is consistent.

They do not describe products.

They define meaning.

Once meaning is controlled, pricing changes.

The question of "why does this cost more?" becomes less relevant because the decision is no longer based on features alone. The customer is not choosing between similar items. The customer is choosing between identities.

This is why a company can sell a product at a multiple of its competitors, even when the underlying cost is similar.

It is not a pricing strategy.

It is a control strategy.

Distribution follows the same principle.

Most companies expand by increasing access. They seek more channels, more sellers, more exposure. First, this creates growth. But without control, that growth introduces inconsistency.

Pricing begins to vary. Presentation changes from one channel to another. The brand appears differently depending on where it is encountered.

Over time, this weakens perception.

Nike, Apple, and Coca-Cola approach distribution differently.

They do not simply expand access. They define it.

Nike limits who can represent the brand and under what conditions. Apple controls the environment in which its products are sold, whether through its own stores or through carefully structured reseller programs. Coca-Cola operates through a system of controlled partners that maintain consistency across markets.

In each case, the objective is not ownership of every channel.

It is control over how the brand exists within those channels.

That distinction determines whether the company directs the market or responds to it.

Another layer of control appears in how these companies build their brands over time.

Most businesses focus on a single name, hoping it will carry all growth. But these companies build systems of brands. They create structures where multiple trademarks operate together, targeting different segments while reinforcing the overall position.

Nike extends into sub-brands that speak to specific audiences. Apple expands its ecosystem while maintaining a unified identity. Coca-Cola controls shelf space and consumer choice through a portfolio of related brands.

This is not expansion by addition.

It is expansion by structure.

Each new brand strengthens the system rather than fragmenting it.

Growth, in most companies, introduces instability.

More products. More markets. More partners.

Each layer adds complexity, and with complexity comes the risk of losing control.

But when the brand is structured correctly, growth reinforces control rather than weakening it.

Nike expands globally while maintaining identity. Apple introduces new products without breaking consistency. Coca-Cola enters new markets while preserving recognition.

The difference is not scale.

It is discipline.

There is also something less visible that separates these companies from others.

They do not spend their time reacting.

They do not rely on constant enforcement to maintain their position. Instead, they create conditions where enforcement becomes less necessary.

Their trademarks are clear. Their presentation is consistent. Their expectations are defined.

As a result, competitors understand the boundaries.

And most choose not to cross them.

This is the shift most companies never make.

They focus on the product. They optimize operations. They pursue short-term growth.

But they never build a structure that allows them to control the environment around what they sell.

And without that structure, they are forced into competition.

Price becomes the primary variable. Distribution becomes unpredictable. Expansion becomes difficult to manage.

They grow, but they do not control what they have built.

The framework used by dominant companies is not complex.

It is simply applied consistently.

They define what their brand represents. They ensure that representation is clear and repeatable. They control who is allowed to use it, where it appears, and how it evolves over time.

And once those elements align, something important happens.

They stop competing in the same way as everyone else.

Closing Observation

They did not win because they were better.
They won because they made comparisons irrelevant.

Part II: Scaling Without Losing Control

Chapter 6

Trademark Licensing: How Smart Companies Turn Brands into Revenue

The Founder saw it as an opportunity he couldn't ignore.

The brand had traction. Sales were steady. More importantly, people were starting to recognize the name without explanation. It carried weight beyond the product itself.

That was when the first proposal came in.

A partner, experienced, well-connected, wanted to use the brand to sell in a new market. They would manage everything. Production, distribution, operations.

All the Founder needed to do was allow the use of the name.

In return, he would receive a percentage of sales.

It felt efficient.

No additional staff.
No capital investment.
No operational burden.

Just expansion.

The agreement was signed. The brand entered a new market. Revenue increased.

Encouraged by the results, the Founder approved another partner. Then another. Each one brought reach. Each one extended the brand further.

From the outside, it looked like scale.

The brand appeared in more places. Sales continued to rise. The business seemed to be growing faster: with less effort.

And for a time, the strategy appeared to be working exactly as intended.

Strategic Principle

"He will win who knows how to manage both superior and inferior forces." Sun Tzu

The strongest position is not doing everything yourself, it is controlling what others do.

Most businesses believe revenue comes from selling products.

They focus on production, logistics, staffing, and operations. Growth is measured by how much more they can build, manage, and deliver.

But there is another way to grow.

A way that separates the act of selling from the act of controlling.

Trademark licensing exists at that intersection.

At its simplest, licensing allows a company to grant others the right to use its brand in exchange for payment. That payment may take the form of royalties, fixed fees, or a combination of both.

But that definition, while accurate, misses the strategic significance.

Licensing is not about letting others use your brand.

It is about controlling how your brand expands.

The shift that licensing creates is subtle, but powerful.

A company that sells products earns revenue from what it produces. A company that licenses its brand earns revenue from what others produce under its control.

The role changes.

From being an operator, to being a controller.

And when that shift is executed correctly, something important happens.

Growth is no longer limited by internal capacity.

It becomes a function of how effectively the brand can be extended.

There is a principle in strategy that appears across many disciplines.

The strongest position is the one that produces results without carrying the full burden.

Licensing reflects that principle directly.

Instead of building infrastructure, hiring teams, and managing expansion internally, the company allows others to do the work, while maintaining control over the brand that makes the work valuable.

From the outside, this can appear effortless.

Revenue increases without visible expansion. Markets are entered without the usual costs. The business seems to grow without the strain that typically accompanies scale.

But this perception hides an important truth.

Licensing is not passive.

It only appears that way when it is done correctly.

At the center of licensing is a balance.

Too little control, and the brand begins to weaken.

Too much control, and the relationship begins to resemble something else entirely: something regulated, structured, and potentially burdensome.

Most companies fail because they move too far in one direction.

Some treat licensing as permission. They allow partners to use the brand with minimal oversight, assuming that growth will reinforce the brand's value. What follows is inconsistency. Products vary. Presentation shifts. Quality becomes uneven.

Over time, the brand stops being something specific.

And when that happens, it begins to lose its function.

Others move in the opposite direction. They try to control not just the brand, but the entire business behind it. They dictate operations, impose strict systems, and blur the line between licensing and franchising.

At that point, the structure changes.

And with that change comes regulation, liability, and complexity that was never intended.

The strategy is not found at either extreme.

It exists in the space between them.

A well-structured licensing system defines boundaries clearly.

It determines what products can be sold under the brand, where those products can appear, and how the brand must be presented. It establishes quality standards that preserve consistency across all uses. And it creates mechanisms for monitoring and enforcement that ensure those standards are maintained.

None of these elements are optional.

They are what allow the brand to expand without losing its meaning.

There is also a tendency to believe that licensing can be applied at any stage.

That is rarely true.

If a brand has not yet established recognition, if it does not carry demand beyond the product itself, licensing becomes difficult to sustain. Partners may struggle to generate results. The brand may fail to differentiate in new markets.

In those situations, expansion does not strengthen the brand.

It exposes its limitations.

When licensing is used at the right time, with the right structure, it creates a different type of growth.

A company can enter new markets without building from the ground up. It can leverage local expertise without losing control. It can increase revenue streams without increasing operational complexity.

But all of that depends on one condition.

The brand must remain consistent.

Not similar. Not approximate.

Consistent.

Because consistency is what allows customers to recognize the brand regardless of where it appears. It is what allows the trademark to carry meaning across different products, markets, and partners.

And without that meaning, licensing becomes nothing more than short-term expansion.

Most companies approach growth by asking a simple question:

"How can we sell more?"

Strategic companies ask a different one:

"How can we control more without doing more?"

Licensing, when understood correctly, answers that question.

But it does so with a requirement that cannot be ignored.

Control must be maintained.

Not occasionally. Not when problems arise.

Continuously.

Closing Observation

It felt like expansion.
He had not yet measured what it was costing him.

Chapter 7

The Licensing Trap: When Your Trademark Deal Becomes a Franchise

The Founder did not set out to build a system.

He set out to protect the brand.

The first licensing agreement had gone well. The partner was competent. The product met expectations. Revenue flowed without the operational burden he once carried himself.

So, when the second deal came, he approached it with more confidence.

This time, he wanted consistency.

He provided clearer guidance. He outlined how the product should be presented. He suggested marketing approaches that had worked before. He shared what he believed would help the partner succeed faster.

It felt responsible.

The partner welcomed the direction. Results improved. The brand appeared more aligned across markets.

Encouraged, the Founder went further.

He created structured materials. He refined messaging. He made expectations more specific. What began as guidance slowly became requirement.

Not all at once.

But step by step.

Each addition made sense on its own.

Each change improved control.

And because the outcomes appeared positive, there was no reason to question the direction.

From the outside, the brand looked stronger than ever.

More consistent. More organized. More scalable.

And for a time, the system appeared to be working exactly as intended.

Strategic Principle

"In the midst of chaos, there is also opportunity." Sun Tzu

The opportunity to control is always present, but so is the risk of overreaching.

Most business owners approach licensing with a simple idea.

They believe they can allow others to use their brand, collect a fee, and expand without taking on additional burden.

At a distance, the model appears clean.

Low cost.
Low risk.
Scalable.

But there is a line embedded within that structure.

A line that is rarely visible at the beginning.

And once it is crossed, the nature of the relationship changes, whether the company intended it or not.

At its core, licensing and franchising are not the same.

Licensing is centered on the brand. It allows another party to use a trademark under defined conditions. The focus is on how the brand appears, how it is represented, and how its meaning is preserved.

Franchising goes further.

It extends control beyond the brand and into the operation of the business itself. It defines systems, processes, and methods. It creates a structure where the brand and the business become inseparable.

The distinction may seem subtle.

In practice, it is not.

The shift does not usually happen in a single moment.

It happens gradually.

A company licenses its brand. It charges a fee. Everything remains within the expected framework.

Then, in an effort to protect consistency, it begins to provide more direction.

Guidance becomes expectation.

Expectation becomes requirement.

And over time, the company is no longer influencing how the brand is used.

It is controlling how the business operates.

In the United States, there is a framework that determines when a relationship may be considered a franchise. It is not based on what the parties call it. It is based on what the relationship actually is.

Three elements tend to define the shift.

The use of a trademark.
The payment of a fee.
And a level of control or assistance that extends into how the business operates.

When those elements come together, the classification may change.

And when the classification changes, the obligations change with it.

This is where the risk becomes real.

Franchises are regulated. They require disclosures. They require compliance with both federal and state frameworks. They introduce liability in ways that licensing does not.

Agreements that were drafted as licenses may no longer function as intended. Relationships that were meant to be flexible become structured. What was designed as a growth strategy becomes a regulatory obligation.

And in many cases, the company never intended to create that outcome.

The difficulty is that control feels necessary.

A company builds a brand and wants to protect it. It wants consistency across markets. It wants to ensure that customers have the same experience regardless of where they encounter the product.

So, it adds structure.

It provides systems.
It defines processes.
It introduces training.

Each step improves alignment.

Each step strengthens control.

But control, when extended beyond the brand itself, begins to change the nature of the relationship.

There is a tension that sits at the center of licensing strategy.

Too little control, and the brand weakens.

Too much control, and the structure shifts into something else entirely.

The objective is not to eliminate that tension.

It is to manage it.

A well-structured licensing system focuses on what must be controlled, and nothing more.

It defines how the brand is used, how quality is maintained, and how consistency is preserved. It sets boundaries that protect the trademark without dictating how the entire business must operate.

It allows partners to run their operations, while requiring that the brand attached to those operations remains intact.

That distinction is what keeps the structure within the intended framework.

There are also signals that indicate when a company is moving too far.

When requirements extend into how a partner runs its daily business. When systems become mandatory rather than optional. When the relationship begins to resemble a complete operational model rather than a brand agreement.

These are not isolated decisions.

They are indicators of a shift.

And that shift carries consequences.

When companies understand this boundary, licensing becomes one of the most powerful tools available.

It allows for expansion without excessive risk. It creates revenue streams without operational strain. It enables growth across markets while maintaining control over what matters.

But when the boundary is ignored, the same structure becomes a source of exposure.

Not because the strategy was flawed.

But because the control was misapplied.

Most companies believe that more control leads to better outcomes.

Strategic companies recognize something more precise.

The right control leads to sustainable growth.

Closing Observation

It didn't change all at once.
He only realized it after the structure had already shifted.

Chapter 8

How Smart Brands Control Pricing Without Breaking the Law

Most business owners want the same thing.

Control over price.

They want consistency across sellers. They want to protect margins. They want to avoid the slow erosion that comes when discounting becomes the primary way products move through the market.

So, they try to fix it.

They tell distributors not to go below a certain number. They pressure resellers to maintain pricing. They react when one seller begins to undercut the rest.

And without realizing it, they move into dangerous territory.

Because in many cases, direct control over resale pricing is not just ineffective.

It creates legal risk.

Strategic Principle

"The skillful leader subdues the enemy's troops without any fighting." Sun Tzu

Do not force the outcome. Shape the conditions so the outcome becomes inevitable.

The instinct to control price is understandable.

Price determines margin. Margin determines sustainability. And in competitive markets, price is often the first variable that begins to move when control is lost.

But pricing, in most systems, is not meant to be dictated.

It is meant to be influenced.

And the distinction between those two approaches determines whether a company maintains control or creates exposure.

There is a concept commonly referred to as resale price maintenance.

At its simplest, it involves requiring resellers to adhere to a fixed or minimum price. In practice, it often appears less direct: pressure, incentives, or informal coordination that attempts to produce the same result.

Regardless of the form, the risk remains.

The more a company attempts to control the price itself, the more it moves into a space where the law begins to intervene.

This is where most businesses approach the problem incorrectly.

They try to control the result.

Smart companies do something different.

They control the environment.

Nike Today: What It Controls (And What It Never Has to Say)

Nike does not tell its retailers what price to sell at.

It does not need to.

Because long before a product reaches the shelf, the conditions that influence pricing have already been established.

Nike controls who are allowed to sell its products. It limits access to retailers that meet its standards. It defines how the brand is presented, how products are released, and how demand is created.

The result is not forced pricing.

It is disciplined pricing.

Retailers understand that access to the brand carries value. That value is not maintained through discounting. It is maintained through alignment.

Nike does not need to enforce pricing directly.

The structure does it for them.

The lesson is not that pricing control is impossible.

It is that pricing control must be indirect.

A company that attempts to dictate price will find resistance: from the market, from its partners, and potentially from the law.

A company that shapes the environment in which pricing occurs will find that the outcome begins to stabilize on its own.

This begins with distribution.

When too many sellers have access to a product, competition becomes internal. Sellers compete against each other rather than against the market. Price becomes the easiest variable to adjust.

And once that begins, it accelerates.

The solution is not to monitor every transaction.

It is to control who is allowed to participate.

Selective distribution limits access to those who meet defined standards. Exclusive structures reduce overlap between sellers. Both approaches reduce the pressure that leads to aggressive discounting.

Pricing stabilizes, not because it is controlled, but because the conditions no longer encourage instability.

Perception plays an even more powerful role.

A brand that is positioned as premium carries expectations. Those expectations influence behavior: not only from customers, but from the sellers themselves.

Retailers are less likely to discount aggressively when doing so undermines the very value that attracts customers. The brand itself creates resistance to price erosion.

This is why luxury brands rarely need to intervene.

The perception does the work.

There are also tools that exist within the legal framework but must be used with precision.

Policies that influence how prices are presented, rather than how they are transacted, can shape visibility without dictating outcome. Decisions about who receives supply, how inventory is allocated, and how incentives are structured can further align behavior without creating direct control.

These mechanisms are subtle.

But when applied consistently, they are effective.

The mistake most companies make is focusing on price as an isolated issue.

They attempt to fix it at the point where it becomes visible.

By that stage, the problem has already formed.

Pricing is not created at the moment of sale.

It is created by the structure that surrounds the product.

Distribution, perception, scarcity, and access all influence how pricing behaves. When those elements are aligned, pricing becomes stable without intervention.

When they are not, no amount of direct control will fix the problem.

The consequence of ignoring this is predictable.

Prices begin to fall. Sellers compete aggressively. Margins compress. The brand begins to appear inconsistent across channels.

And over time, the product becomes a commodity.

Not because it changed.

But because the system around it did.

Most businesses approach pricing with a simple question:

"How do we control what others charge?"

Strategic companies ask a different one:

"How do we design a system where pricing takes care of itself?"

Closing Observation

They never controlled the price.
They made it unnecessary to change it.

Chapter 9

Why Your Trademark Should Not Be Owned by Your Operating Company

Most business owners place everything in one place.

The operations, the revenue, the employees, the contracts, and the brand.

It feels efficient. It feels organized. It feels like the simplest way to build.

And in the early stages, it works.

There is no visible problem. The business grows. The brand gains recognition. Revenue begins to stabilize.

From the outside, the structure appears sound.

But structure is not tested during growth.

It is tested when something goes wrong.

Strategic Principle

"He who occupies the field of battle first and awaits his enemy is at ease." Sun Tzu

Position determines outcome long before conflict appears.

There is a basic principle in strategy that applies across disciplines.

You do not place your most valuable asset in your most exposed position.

In most businesses, however, that is exactly what happens.

The operating company, the entity that signs contracts, hires employees, interacts with customers, and absorbs risk, is also the entity that holds the trademark.

The same structure that creates value is the structure that is exposed to loss.

At first, this does not appear to matter.

The business functions. The brand grows. The distinction between operations and ownership seems unnecessary.

But the distinction exists whether it is acknowledged or not.

And over time, it becomes critical.

An operating company is designed to function.

It engages with the market. It enters into agreements. It takes on obligations. It carries liability as a natural consequence of activity.

It is, by design, exposed.

A trademark is different.

It does not conduct operations. It does not enter into day-to-day transactions. It does not absorb the same level of risk.

What it carries is value.

It defines how customers recognize the business. It supports pricing. It enables expansion. It becomes the asset that others evaluate when the company is reviewed from the outside.

When both are placed in the same structure, exposure and value become indistinguishable.

And when something affects one, it affects both.

The alternative is not complexity for its own sake.

It is separation with intention.

Strategic companies distinguish between the entity that operates and the entity that owns the brand. The operating company continues to run the business. It generates revenue. It manages the day-to-day functions.

A separate entity holds the trademark.

The relationship between them is defined, not assumed. The operating company uses the brand under a license. The terms of that use are controlled. The value remains anchored in the entity that is not directly exposed to operational risk.

This is not an abstract concept.

It is a structural decision that affects control, protection, and long-term value.

The impact of this separation becomes visible in several ways.

First, it protects the asset.

If the operating company faces a dispute, a liability event, or financial pressure, the trademark is not automatically part of that exposure. The brand remains intact, even if the operating structure encounters difficulty.

Second, it defines control.

The entity that owns the trademark controls how it is used. It sets the conditions under which the brand appears in the market. It determines how expansion occurs, and under what terms others may participate.

Control does not follow effort.

It follows ownership.

Third, it creates flexibility.

A trademark held separately can be licensed, expanded, or leveraged without being tied directly to the operational structure. It can support new markets, new partnerships, and new revenue streams without requiring the entire business to shift.

This is where licensing, expansion, and strategic growth begin to align.

Because the brand is not trapped within the operations.

It can move.

Fourth, it affects valuation.

When a business is evaluated, by an investor, a partner, or a buyer, the clarity of ownership becomes central. The question is not simply whether the company generates revenue. It is whether the asset driving that revenue is clearly defined, transferable, and scalable.

If the trademark sits within a structure that is exposed, unclear, or difficult to separate, the perceived risk increases.

And when risk increases, value decreases.

The mistake most companies make is assuming that structure can be addressed later.

That it can be reorganized when the business grows, when investment becomes relevant, or when a sale is considered.

But restructuring is rarely simple once the business has scale.

Ownership becomes layered. Tax considerations emerge. Agreements must be adjusted. What could have been designed early becomes difficult to unwind.

And by that stage, the cost of correction is significantly higher.

There are also errors that arise even when companies attempt to implement this structure.

Separation without documentation creates confusion rather than clarity. Entities are formed without clear purpose. Agreements are implied rather than defined.

Structure, without precision, produces the same outcome as no structure at all.

The objective is not to create complexity.

It is to create clarity.

At its core, the decision is simple.

The operating company carries risk.

The trademark carries value.

Placing both in the same structure ties value to risk in a way that is rarely intentional.

Separating them allows each to function as it should.

Most business owners approach structure with the goal of simplicity.

Strategic operators approach it with the goal of control.

They recognize that where the trademark sits determines who controls the business, how it can expand, and what it is worth when evaluated.

And once that is understood, the decision becomes less about convenience and more about position.

Closing Observation

He built the business inside the risk.
The asset never needed to be there.

Chapter 10

Why Buyers Pay More for Companies with Strong Trademarks

Most business owners believe value is created through effort.

They focus on revenue, profit, operations, and growth. They assume that if those numbers are strong enough, the valuation will follow.

Those elements matter.

But they are not what drives premium outcomes.

When a serious buyer evaluates a company, the question is not what has been built.

It is what will remain.

Strategic Principle

> *"Victorious warriors win first and then go to war."* Sun Tzu

The outcome is decided before the negotiation begins.

A buyer is not paying for history.

They are paying for continuity.

They want to know whether the business can continue generating revenue if ownership changes, if operations evolve, or if market conditions shift.

They want to know what survives.

And the answer almost always comes down to one thing.

The brand.

Products can be replaced.

Operations can be restructured.

Teams can be rebuilt.

But a strong brand carries something that is far more difficult to replicate.

Recognition.

Trust.

Position.

These do not disappear when ownership changes.

They transfer.

And because they transfer, they become the foundation of value.

Arnault Today: What He Owns (And What Others Try to Build)

Bernard Arnault does not build value the way most companies do.

He does not compete in volume. He does not rely on discounting. He does not expand by making products more accessible.

He controls something else entirely.

Perception.

The brands under his control (Louis Vuitton, Dior, and others) do not dominate because of manufacturing advantages. They dominate because of what they stand for.

Scarcity. Identity. Status.

Arnault does not allow these brands to be diluted through uncontrolled distribution. Access is limited. Presentation is controlled. Pricing is protected: not by direct enforcement, but by the structure surrounding the brand.

As a result, the products are not compared in the same way as others.

They exist in a different category.

And when a business operates in a category it defines, valuation changes.

Because the buyer is no longer purchasing a product line.

They are acquiring control over perception.

This is why, in many transactions, the largest portion of value is not assigned to physical assets.

It is assigned to intangible ones.

The trademark, the goodwill attached to it, and the position it holds in the market often represent the majority of what is being acquired.

Not because they are abstract.

But because they determine what happens next.

A strong trademark supports pricing in a way that operations cannot.

When a brand is trusted, customers do not evaluate it against every alternative. They make decisions based on expectation.

That expectation stabilizes revenue.

And stable revenue supports valuation.

The same principle applies to growth.

A business that relies entirely on marketing to generate demand carries a different risk profile than one where the brand itself drives recognition.

When the brand carries weight, expansion becomes easier. New products gain traction faster. New markets require less effort.

From a buyer's perspective, this represents opportunity.

Not theoretical opportunity, but practical, repeatable growth.

Predictability also becomes visible.

Revenue driven by brand loyalty behaves differently than revenue driven by constant acquisition. It repeats. It stabilizes. It reduces volatility.

And when volatility is reduced, risk decreases.

Reduced risk increases value.

At the same time, a strong trademark creates distance from competitors.

It becomes more difficult for others to replicate the position. The brand defines a space that is not easily entered without creating confusion.

This reduces direct competition.

And when competition is reduced, control increases.

The opposite is equally important.

Weak trademarks introduce uncertainty.

If ownership is unclear, if the brand is inconsistent, if similar marks exist, or if enforcement has been inconsistent, the buyer begins to question the asset.

Not because the business lacks revenue.

But because the revenue may not be protected.

And when protection is uncertain, value declines quickly.

This is why deals often shift during due diligence.

Not because revenue changed.

But because clarity did.

Ownership is examined. Strength is tested. Scope is evaluated. Risk is identified.

And in that moment, the true position of the business becomes visible.

There is a principle in strategy that applies directly here.

The outcome is determined before the negotiation begins.

If the trademark is strong, clean, and controlled, the negotiation reflects that strength. The buyer is trying to secure an asset.

If it is weak or unclear, the negotiation becomes defensive. Risk is identified, price is adjusted, and the structure of the deal shifts accordingly.

The same company can produce different outcomes based on this single factor.

Most businesses try to increase value by increasing revenue.

Strategic companies increase value by strengthening brands.

Because revenue can fluctuate.

But a strong trademark carries forward.

In the end, a buyer is not buying what has been built.

They are buying what will continue.

They are evaluating whether the brand can sustain pricing, support expansion, and keep its position under new ownership.

If it can, value increases.

If it cannot, value declines, regardless of past performance.

Closing Observation

The numbers supported the deal.
The brand justified the price.

Part III: Strategic Execution

Chapter 11

Trademark Classes: How to File Strategically (Not Expensively)

Most business owners ask the same question at the beginning of the trademark process.

How many classes do I need?

It sounds like the right place to start. It feels practical. It suggests that the answer will determine how well the brand is protected.

But it is the wrong question.

The real question is different.

How do you protect your business without wasting money?

Strategic Principle

"He will win who knows what to fight and what not to fight." Sun Tzu

You do not protect everything. You protect what matters.

A trademark does not protect a name everywhere.

It protects a name in specific categories.

Those categories are called classes.

Each class represents a defined group of goods or services. Clothing falls into one class. Software into another. Retail services into yet another. When a trademark is filed, it is not attached to the name alone, it is attached to the name within those categories.

This distinction is where most mistakes begin.

Because once a business understands that protection is limited to where the trademark is filed, the instinct is to expand that protection as broadly as possible.

More classes feel safer.

More classes feel like stronger protection.

But that assumption creates its own problem.

Filing too many classes does not necessarily strengthen a trademark.

It increases cost. Each class carries its own filing fee. It increases maintenance obligations. Each class must eventually be supported by use. And if that use cannot be demonstrated, the protection weakens or disappears entirely.

Protection that cannot be supported is not protection.

It is exposure.

The opposite mistake is just as common.

Some businesses file in a single class, the most obvious one, and stop there. They assume that protecting the product itself is sufficient.

At first, this appears to work.

The product is covered. The name is registered. The business moves forward.

But the market does not operate within a single category.

Customers do not interact with a brand in only one way. They encounter it through products, through services, through platforms, through distribution channels that extend beyond the initial filing.

And this is where gaps begin to appear.

A company may protect its product, but not the way it sells that product. It may secure the name for manufacturing, but not for retail. It may establish a position in one category, while leaving adjacent categories open.

Those openings are rarely obvious at the beginning.

They become visible when someone else steps into them.

Strategic filing does not begin with classes.

It begins with the business itself.

Where does the company generate value?

Not just what it sells, but how it sells it.

A business that manufactures a product operates differently from one that sells directly to consumers. A company that builds a platform carries a different set of risks than one that provides services. A brand that intends to expand through licensing or franchising requires a broader structure than one that remains limited to a single channel.

The trademark must reflect that reality.

This is where the focus shifts.

Instead of asking how many classes are needed, the question becomes where the brand operates and where it is going.

A business that sells physical products may require protection in the category of the product itself, but also in the category that covers how those products are offered to the public. A software company may need protection not only for the software, but for the services surrounding it. A brand that intends to scale may need to consider how its name will function across multiple layers of interaction.

The objective is not to predict every possible future.

It is to protect the path.

There is a tendency to treat trademark filings as static.

A one-time decision that remains fixed as the business grows.

But growth changes the structure of the business.

New products are introduced. New services emerge. New channels are developed. And each of these creates a new point of interaction between the brand and the market.

If the trademark does not evolve with that structure, gaps form.

And those gaps are where risk accumulates.

Cost is often what drives the initial decision.

Each additional class increases the expense. And for many businesses, especially early on, controlling cost is a priority.

But cost alone is not the correct measure.

The question is not how much the filing costs.

It is how well the filing aligns with the business.

A poorly aligned trademark, whether overextended or too narrow, creates expenses later that far exceed the initial savings.

Strategic operators approach this differently.

They identify where revenue is generated. They understand how customers interact with the brand. They consider how the business is expected to expand.

And then they align protection with those realities.

Not everything is covered.

But everything that matters is.

There are also boundaries that must be respected.

Trademark law does not allow a company to block entire markets without basis. Protection must be tied to actual use or a legitimate intent to use. Filing in categories with no connection to the business creates risk rather than strength.

The goal is not to claim territory.

It is to define it.

Over time, the structure of a trademark portfolio becomes a reflection of the business itself.

Clear, aligned filings indicate a company that understands its position. Scattered, inconsistent filings suggest the opposite.

And when that portfolio is reviewed, whether by a partner, an investor, or a buyer, it communicates more than the name alone.

It communicates strategy.

Most business owners believe that more protection is better.

Strategic operators understand something more precise.

Targeted protection is stronger.

Because it is supported.

Because it is enforceable.

And because it reflects the way the business operates.

Closing Observation

He filed for what he saw.
The risk was in what he did not.

Chapter 12

How to Choose a Strong Trademark Name That Competitors Cannot Touch

Most founders spend significant time building their product.

They refine features. They adjust pricing. They test the market. They invest energy into everything that feels tangible.

Then they choose a name.

Often quickly.

Often based on what feels clear, descriptive, or easy to understand.

And without realizing it, they make one of the most important strategic decisions in the entire business, with the least amount of thought.

Strategic Principle

> *"If you know the enemy and know yourself, you need not fear the result of a hundred battles."* Sun Tzu

The strongest position is chosen before competition begins.

A name is not branding.

It is not a label.

It is a position.

From a legal and strategic perspective, not all names are equal. Some create immediate limitations. Others create space. And the difference between them determines how easily a brand can be protected, how clearly it can be enforced, and how far it can expand.

Most businesses choose names that describe what they do.

It feels logical. It feels efficient. A descriptive name communicates the product or service immediately. It reduces friction in understanding.

But what it gains in clarity, it loses control.

A name that describes the product cannot be owned in the same way as a name that stands apart from it. Competitors can move closer. Variations become harder to distinguish. Enforcement becomes more difficult.

And over time, the brand blends into the market rather than defining a position within it.

From a legal standpoint, names fall into different categories.

At the lowest end are generic terms: names that describe the product itself. These cannot be protected. They belong to the market, not to any one business.

Slightly above are descriptive names: terms that describe qualities, features, or characteristics. These can sometimes be protected, but only with difficulty, and only after significant use. Even then, the protection is limited.

At the other end there are names that do not describe the product at all.

These are the names that create power.

They may suggest something indirectly. They may use familiar words in unfamiliar ways. Or they may be entirely invented. In each case, the name does not compete within the category.

It defines it.

Jobs Today: What He Chose (And What Others Avoid)

When Steve Jobs chose the name Apple, he did not choose clarity.

He chose control.

The name did not describe computers. It did not reference technology. It did not explain what the company produced.

And that was precisely the advantage.

Because the name carried no predefined meaning, the company was free to define it. Over time, Apple became associated with simplicity, design, and experience: not because the name explained those qualities, but because the company built them into the brand.

If the name had been descriptive, that control would have been limited.

Competitors could have approached it more closely. Variations would have been harder to distinguish. The brand would have existed within a category rather than above it.

By choosing a name that stood apart, Jobs created distance before competition even began.

This is the shift most founders never make.

They choose names based on immediate understanding.

Strategic operators choose names based on long-term control.

A strong name does something subtle but powerful.

It reduces the number of conflicts before they occur.

Competitors avoid names that are clearly distinct. The boundaries are easier to recognize. The risk of infringement is more visible.

As a result, fewer challenges arise.

And when they do, they are easier to resolve.

A weak name produces the opposite effect.

It invites similarity. It allows competitors to operate close to the brand without clearly crossing a line. It creates ambiguity.

And ambiguity is expensive.

It leads to disputes. It increases legal costs. It weakens enforcement. It forces the company to spend time explaining what should have been obvious.

There is also a longer-term effect that is often overlooked.

Expansion.

A descriptive name ties a company to what it does today. It limits how far the brand can extend. A business that begins with a narrow description often finds itself constrained when it attempts to grow beyond that description.

A strong name does not carry that limitation.

It can expand across products, services, and markets without losing relevance.

Because it was never tied to a single function.

There is a common misconception that descriptive names are necessary for visibility.

That customers need to understand immediately what the company does.

But visibility does not come from the name alone.

It comes from how the name is used, how it is positioned, and how it is reinforced over time.

A strong name builds meaning.

A weak name explains function.

Only one of those creates long-term advantage.

Choosing a name, then, is not a creative exercise.

It is a strategic decision.

It determines how easily the brand can be protected. It defines how close competitors can get. It influences how the business expands. And it shapes how the market perceives the company before any interaction occurs.

Most founders approach this decision by asking what sounds right.

Strategic founders ask a different question.

What can we own?

Closing Observation

The name did not explain the business.
It made the business harder to compete with.

Chapter 13

Intent-to-Use vs. Actual Use: The Trademark Strategy Most Founders Get Wrong

Most founders believe filing a trademark is a simple step.

They have a name. They plan to use it. And at some point, they assume they will register it.

The timing, in their view, is flexible.

It is something that can be handled once the product is ready, once the business is launched, or once revenue begins to appear.

That assumption creates one of the most common, and costly, mistakes in trademark strategy.

Because in this system, timing is not a detail.

It is the position.

Strategic Principle

"Victorious warriors win first, then go to war." Sun Tzu

Secure your position before the market sees you.

In the United States, there are two primary ways to file a trademark.

One is based on actual use. The other is based on intent to use.

At a surface level, the distinction seems straightforward.

Actual use means the brand is already in the market. Products are being sold. Services are being offered. The name is publicly tied to commercial activity.

Intent-to-use means the brand is not yet in use. The product is still being developed. The launch has not occurred. The business is preparing to enter the market.

But beneath that distinction is something far more important.

Control over timing.

Trademark law does not reward ideas.

It rewards position.

And position, in many cases, is determined by who files first.

Not who thought of the name first. Not who spent more time developing the concept. Not who intended to build the business.

The system recognizes action.

And filing is that action.

This is where most founders hesitate.

They wait until the product is complete. They wait until the brand feels ready. They wait until they are confident in the direction of the business.

Meanwhile, the market remains open.

And open space invites movement.

Another party may file. Another party may begin using a similar name. And once that happens, the position shifts, often permanently.

The founder who waited is no longer establishing control.

They are reacting.

Intent-to-use exists to prevent that outcome.

It allows a business to secure its position before entering the market. It creates a priority date that reflects intent backed by action. It signals that the name is being claimed, even before it is visible to the public.

In practical terms, it buys time.

But it does not remove responsibility.

An intent-to-use application is not a placeholder without consequence.

It carries requirements.

The intent must be genuine. The plan to use the mark must be real. And within a defined period, that use must materialize. The system allows preparation, but not indefinite delay.

If the brand is never used, the application does not survive.

This is where misuse often occurs.

Some founders file broadly, claiming categories that extend far beyond their actual plans. Others file without a clear timeline, assuming they will figure out the business later.

In both cases, the filing creates the appearance of control, but lacks the substance to support it.

And when the system requires proof, the position weakens.

Actual use, on the other hand, reflects a different stage.

The business is already operating. The brand is already visible. The connection between the name and the product or service is established.

In those situations, filing based on actual use can be more direct. The path to registration is often shorter. The evidence is already in place.

But it carries a limitation.

The position is defined by the moment of use.

If another party has filed earlier, even if they have not yet launched, the earlier filing may control priority.

This is where the misunderstanding becomes clear.

Being in the market does not always mean being in control.

The real strategy is not choosing one method over the other.

It is aligning the method with the stage of the business.

In early development, when the brand has been chosen but not yet launched, intent-to-use creates leverage. It secures the name before exposure. It allows the business to move forward with confidence.

At launch, when the brand enters the market, that position is reinforced through actual use. The application progresses. Protection becomes enforceable.

As the business expands, additional filings may be required to reflect new products, services, or markets.

In this way, trademark strategy is not a single event.

It is a sequence.

The risk appears when that sequence is ignored.

When filing is delayed, priority can be lost. When intent is not supported by action, applications can fail. When use is inconsistent or unclear, protection weakens.

None of these issues are visible at the beginning.

They become visible when the position is tested.

There is a tendency to believe that trademarks are about registration.

In reality, they are about timing.

The moment a name becomes visible, the competition begins, not only in the market, but in the system that determines who controls that name.

The companies that understand this do not wait for certainty.

They act before exposure.

Most founders think:

"We will file when we are ready."

Strategic operators think differently.

They understand that readiness is not the trigger.

Position is.

Closing Observation

He waited until the brand was ready.
The position was already taken.

Chapter 14

Trademark Search: Why Most Searches Miss the Real Risk

Most founders believe a trademark search is straightforward.

They type the name into a search engine. They check a database. They look for an exact match. And if nothing obvious appears, they move forward.

It feels logical.

If no one is using the exact name, the assumption is that the name is available.

That assumption is where many problems begin.

Strategic Principle

> *"If you know the enemy and know yourself, you need not fear the result of a hundred battles."* Sun Tzu

The greatest advantage comes from seeing what others overlook.

Trademark risk is rarely obvious.

It does not sit in plain view, waiting to be discovered through a simple search. It exists in the space around what is visible: in similarities, patterns, and relationships that are not immediately clear.

Most searches are designed to find what is identical.

Trademark law is concerned with what is confusing.

This distinction changes everything.

A conflict does not require two names to be the same. It requires them to be similar enough that a customer could reasonably believe they come from the same source.

Similarity can take many forms.

It can be visual: names that look alike at a glance. It can be phonetic: names that sound alike when spoken. It can be conceptual: names that suggest the same idea or meaning.

None of these require an exact match.

And because of that, they are often missed.

A basic search reveals what is obvious.

It does not reveal what is dangerous.

Search engines prioritize visibility, not legal relevance. Databases can identify identical or near-identical entries, but they do not interpret risk. Automated tools can produce results quickly, but they lack judgment.

They collect information.

They do not analyze it.

This creates a false sense of security.

A founder runs a search. Nothing appears that seems directly conflicting. The name feels available. The process moves forward.

Only later, sometimes months, sometimes years, does the issue surface.

An application is refused. A notice is received. A competitor challenges the use.

At that point, the problem is no longer theoretical.

It is operational.

The core issue is that trademark conflict is not about ownership alone.

It is about likelihood of confusion.

That standard is broader than most expect. It considers how the name appears, how it sounds, how it is used, and where it exists in the market. It evaluates whether two brands could reasonably be associated with each other, even if they are not identical.

This is why a name can appear available and still carry risk.

A proper search does not begin with the question, "Is this name taken?"

It begins with a different question.

How risky is this name?

Answering that question requires more than collecting data.

It requires interpretation.

Similar marks must be identified, not just identical ones. Related industries must be considered, not just identical categories. The strength of existing marks must be evaluated, because not all trademarks carry the same weight.

Some are narrow. Some are broad. Some are weak. Some are highly enforceable.

The difference matters.

There is also a layer of risk that does not appear in formal records.

Unregistered use.

Businesses can operate under names that are not formally registered but still carry rights within a geographic area or market. These uses may not appear in official databases, but they can still create conflict.

This is where many searches fail completely.

They rely on what is recorded, not on what is used.

Timing introduces another dimension.

A name may appear clear today, but another party may have already filed an application that has not yet become visible. When that application surfaces, it may establish priority that predates the search.

What appeared to be open space was already claimed.

These layers, similarity, related markets, unregistered use, and timing, combine to create a risk profile that is not immediately visible.

And this is why superficial searches create deeper problems.

The cost of getting this wrong is rarely limited to the search itself.

If a conflict is identified during the application process, time is lost. If the issue arises after the brand has been built, the consequences are more severe.

Rebranding becomes necessary.

Materials must be replaced. Recognition must be rebuilt. Momentum is disrupted.

In some cases, legal disputes follow.

And in all cases, the cost exceeds what would have been required to evaluate the risk properly at the beginning.

There is a principle in strategy that applies directly here.

The outcome is determined before you enter the field.

A company that understands the landscape before committing to a name moves with confidence. A company that does not is forced to react.

The goal of a trademark search is not certainty.

Certainty does not exist.

The goal is clarity.

To understand where the risks are, how significant they are, and whether the name is worth defending over time.

Some risks are manageable. Others are not.

The distinction must be made early.

Most founders approach the process by asking whether a name is available.

Strategic operators ask a different question.

Whether the name is defensible.

Closing Observation

Nothing appeared in the search.
The conflict was never meant to.

Chapter 15

How to Build a Brand That Can Be Licensed (Before You Try to License It)

Most business owners believe licensing begins with an agreement.

A contract is drafted. Terms are negotiated. Rights are granted.

From the outside, it is a transaction.

But licensing does not begin with a contract.

It begins much earlier, with how the brand is built.

Strategic Principle

> *"He who wishes to fight must first count the cost."* Sun Tzu

Expansion appears simple, until you realize what must be controlled.

Not every brand can be licensed.

And attempting to force licensing too early does not create growth.

It exposes weakness.

A brand that lacks structure cannot be extended without losing consistency. A brand that depends entirely on the founder cannot be replicated. A brand that has not defined what it represents cannot be carried into new markets by someone else.

Licensing does not solve these problems.

It reveals them.

There is a misconception that licensing is simply a way to do less work.

That a company can step back, allow others to operate, and collect revenue while the brand expands.

But licensing does not reduce responsibility.

It redistributes it.

And without structure, that redistribution leads to fragmentation.

A licensable brand is not defined by recognition alone.

It is defined by clarity.

It must stand for something specific. Not in a general sense, but in a way that can be understood and applied consistently by someone who did not build it.

If the brand represents performance, that standard must be clear. If it represents simplicity, that must be reflected in how products are designed and presented. If it represents luxury, every element, from materials to messaging, must align with that position.

Because a licensee is not creating the brand.

They are executing it.

Consistency is the second requirement.

A brand that appears differently across products, platforms, or markets cannot be licensed effectively. Variations introduce uncertainty. Uncertainty weakens recognition. And without recognition, the value of the trademark begins to erode.

Consistency is not aesthetic.

It is structural.

It ensures that the brand carries the same meaning regardless of where it appears.

Standards follow naturally.

A brand that can be licensed must define what is acceptable and what is not. It must establish quality levels, presentation requirements, and usage rules that preserve its identity.

Without standards, control is lost.

Not immediately.

But gradually, as each licensee interprets the brand in their own way.

There is also a deeper requirement, one that is often overlooked.

The brand must be transferable.

It must function outside the direct control of the founder.

If the business only works because of the person running it, because of decisions made in real time, because of knowledge that has not been documented, because of processes that exist only in practice, then it cannot be licensed.

It can only be operated.

Licensing requires separation.

The system must stand on its own.

Knight Today: What He Built (And What Others Miss)

Phil Knight did not build Nike by controlling every product directly.

He built a system.

The brand represented performance, identity, and aspiration. But that meaning was not left to interpretation. It was reinforced through consistency: across products, across markets, and across every point of contact with the customer.

Manufacturing was distributed. Partnerships were formed. The physical product moved through multiple hands.

But the brand did not change.

Because the system behind it was clear.

Guidelines defined how the brand appeared. Standards ensured that quality remained consistent. The message remained aligned regardless of where the product was sold.

Nike did not license chaos.

It extended a controlled system.

This is where most licensing attempts fail.

Not because the idea is wrong.

But because the foundation is incomplete.

A business may have a product, a name, and even some level of recognition. But without structure, those elements cannot be extended without distortion.

And distortion reduces value.

Timing also plays a role.

Licensing too early creates strain.

If demand has not been established, licensees struggle to generate results. If the brand has not been defined, they interpret it inconsistently. If the system has not been built, they improvise.

In each case, the outcome is the same.

The brand weakens.

The correct sequence is different.

The brand is defined first.

The system is built.

Consistency is established.

Demand is created.

Only then does licensing become effective.

There is a principle in strategy that applies directly here.

Control must exist before expansion.

Without it, growth introduces instability rather than strength.

Most businesses approach licensing by asking how they can grow faster.

Strategic companies ask a different question.

Whether what they have built can be repeated without them.

Because that is the real test.

If the brand were handed to someone else today, would they know what to do?

Would they be able to deliver the same experience?

Would the brand remain consistent?

If the answer is no, the business is not ready to be licensed.

Licensing, when done correctly, is one of the most powerful tools in business.

It allows a company to expand without carrying the full operational burden. It creates additional revenue streams. It increases the reach of the brand across markets.

But it only works when the brand is built to support it.

In the end, a company is not licensing a product.

It is a licensing system.

And if that system is not defined, controlled, and consistent, it will not scale.

It will break.

Closing Observation

They tried to scale the brand.
The system was never built to carry it.

Chapter 16

Cease and Desist Letters: When to Send One, and When Not To

Most business owners see a cease-and-desist letter as the first step.

They discover a competitor using a similar name. They notice a product that feels too close. They see something that crosses a line.

And the instinct is immediate.

Act.

Send a letter. Demand that it stop. Protect the brand.

It feels like the right response.

But it is rarely the right first move.

Strategic Principle

"He will win who knows when to fight and when not to fight." Sun Tzu

The strongest position is not reacting quickly; it is acting at the right moment.

A cease-and-desist letter is not simply communication.

It is a signal.

It tells the other side that you have identified their activity, that you believe it crosses a boundary, and that you are prepared to enforce your position.

Once that signal is sent, the situation changes.

The other side becomes aware. They begin to evaluate their position. They may adjust, respond, or escalate.

In other words, the moment the letter is sent, the interaction becomes active.

This is why timing matters.

Sending a letter too early can weaken your position. Sending it too late can allow damage to spread.

The objective is not to act quickly.

It is to act when the position is clear.

Most mistakes occur because enforcement is driven by emotion.

Frustration leads to action. The desire to stop the behavior immediately overrides the need to evaluate whether the action will be effective.

This produces letters that are poorly structured, overstated, or unsupported.

And once a weak position is communicated, it cannot be taken back.

Credibility, once reduced, is difficult to restore.

A strong enforcement action begins before the letter is written.

It begins with assessment.

Is there actual confusion in the market? Is the use of the mark similar enough to create a problem? Is the industry related? Is the trademark itself strong, consistent, and clearly defined?

These questions are not formalities.

They determine whether the position can be sustained.

There is also a practical consideration that is often overlooked.

A cease-and-desist letter creates an expectation.

If the demand is not followed by action, when necessary, the signal loses strength. Future enforcement becomes more difficult. The perception of the brand's boundaries begins to weaken.

In simple terms, if you are not prepared to follow through, the letter should not be sent.

Not every situation requires a letter.

Some situations require observation.

Monitoring allows a company to gather information, understand patterns, and evaluate whether the issue is isolated or expanding. Acting too early, without that understanding, can create unnecessary conflict.

There are also situations where alternative tools are more effective.

Platform-based enforcement, for example, can resolve certain issues more quickly than direct communication. In other cases, negotiation or coexistence may produce a better outcome than confrontation.

The choice of tool matters as much as the decision to act.

There are risks that arise when a cease-and-desist letter is used incorrectly.

The most immediate is escalation.

The other party may respond aggressively. They may involve counsel. They may challenge the position directly. What could have been managed quietly becomes a dispute.

There is also the risk of weakening the position itself.

If the claims are overstated, unsupported, or inconsistent with actual use, the other side may recognize the weakness. At that point, the dynamic shifts.

The letter no longer controls the situation.

It exposes it.

In some cases, the consequences extend further.

The recipient of a letter may take proactive steps to secure their own position. They may initiate proceedings. They may choose a forum that is more favorable to them. They may move the dispute into a space where control is no longer in your hands.

All of this can begin with a single action taken too early or without preparation.

A strong cease and desist letter does not rely on force.

It relies on clarity.

The position is defined precisely. The infringement is identified without exaggeration. The demand is direct but controlled. The tone is firm, but not emotional.

It communicates readiness without inviting unnecessary conflict.

Timing remains the central factor.

When the infringement is clear, when the impact is real, and when the company is prepared to act, the letter becomes effective. It can resolve issues quickly. It can prevent further damage. It can reinforce the boundaries of the brand.

When those conditions are not present, the same letter creates the opposite effect.

There is a principle in strategy that applies directly here.

Not every battle needs to be fought.

And the strongest position is not created by constant action.

It is created by selective action.

Most businesses believe enforcement means acting immediately.

Strategic operators understand something more precisely.

It means acting correctly.

Closing Observation

He moved to stop the problem.
He had not yet secured the position.

Chapter 17

How to Expand Your Trademark Internationally Without Wasting Money

Most business owners assume that trademark protection can be extended globally.

They build a brand, establish a position in their home market, and then begin to consider expansion. At that point, the instinct is straightforward.

Protect everything.

Register the trademark everywhere. Cover as many countries as possible. Secure the brand before someone else does.

It sounds logical.

It is also one of the fastest ways to waste money.

Strategic Principle

> *"He who knows the terrain and the weather will be victorious."* Sun Tzu

Every market is different. Winning depends on knowing where to move and where not to.

There is no such thing as a global trademark.

Trademark rights are territorial. They exist within the boundaries of individual countries. A registration in one jurisdiction does not automatically extend to another.

A brand protected in the United States is not protected in Europe. It is not protected in China. It is not protected anywhere else unless action is taken in those specific locations.

This is the first reality that shapes international strategy.

If you do not file in a country, you do not control your brand there.

The mistake most companies make is responding to this reality with excess.

They attempt to cover every market. They file in multiple jurisdictions without a clear plan. They assume that broad protection equals strong protection.

But protection without strategy is not strength.

International filings carry cost, not only at the beginning, but over time.

Each country requires its own process. Each registration must be maintained. Renewals must be managed. In some jurisdictions, use must be demonstrated to keep the registration alive.

Filing broadly without a clear purpose creates a portfolio that is expensive to maintain and difficult to manage.

And in many cases, most of those registrations are never used.

The correct question is not where you *can* file.

It is where you *should* file.

Strategic expansion begins with identifying where the business operates or will operate in the near future.

Where is revenue generated?

Where is growth planned?

Where are competitors active?

These questions define priority.

A market that generates revenue deserves protection. A market that is part of a near-term expansion plan requires attention. A market where competitors are active may present risk.

Other markets can wait.

Risk is not evenly distributed.

Some countries operate under first-to-file systems, where the first party to register a mark gains priority, regardless of prior use elsewhere. In those environments, delay can create immediate problems.

A brand that is established in one country may be registered by another party in a different jurisdiction before the original owner enters that market.

When that happens, expansion becomes complicated.
M
ko

In some cases, it becomes blocked.

Timing, then, becomes critical.

Filing too early creates unnecessary cost. Filing too late creates exposure.

The objective is not to move everywhere.

It is to move first where it matters.

There are systems designed to simplify international filing.

The Madrid Protocol allows a company to submit a single application and extend it to multiple countries. At first glance, it appears to offer a unified solution.

But the simplicity is procedural.

Not substantive.

Each country still examines the application independently. Each country applies to its own standards. Each enforces rights within its own system.

The filing may be centralized.

The protection is not.

This is where misunderstandings often occur.

Companies treat international filing as a single event. They submit an application, designate multiple countries, and assume the brand is protected globally.

They have initiated multiple processes.

Each with its own outcome.

There are also practical risks that extend beyond the filing itself.

In some jurisdictions, trademark squatters actively monitor foreign brands. They register marks before the original owner enters the market, anticipating that the brand will eventually need to be acquired.

This creates leverage.

And when the original company attempts to expand, it must negotiate to reclaim what it assumed was already its own.

Language introduces another layer.

A brand that works in one market may not translate effectively into another. Pronunciation may change. Meaning may shift. Variations may emerge that create new risks or new opportunities.

Without consideration of these factors, a company may protect the original name while leaving related versions exposed.

Enforcement also varies.

Each country applies its own rules, procedures, and timelines. What is effective in one jurisdiction may not produce the same result in another. A strategy that works domestically does not always translate directly.

This is why international protection is not simply an extension of domestic strategy.

It is its own system.

There is a sequence that successful companies follow.

They build strength in their primary market. They establish a clear, consistent brand. They define ownership and control.

Then they expand.

Not everywhere.

But into markets that align with their growth.

Over time, they extend protection as the business evolves. Each new filing reflects a deliberate decision, not a defensive reaction.

Most businesses approach international trademarks with a mindset of coverage.

They attempt to protect as much as possible.

Strategic companies approach it with a mindset of position.

They protect what matters.

At the right time.

Closing Observation

They tried to protect everything.
They had not decided where they were going.

Chapter 18

Trademark Infringement: What Actually Matters in Court (Not What You Think)

Most business owners believe trademark infringement is simple.

They see another company using a similar name, and the conclusion feels immediate.

They used my name.

So, I win.

That assumption is understandable.

It is also incorrect.

Strategic Principle

> *"He will win who knows the enemy and knows himself."* Sun Tzu

Victory depends on understanding how the market sees both sides, not how you see yourself.

Trademark disputes are not decided by frustration.

They are not decided by who feels wronged, who invested more effort, or who tells the better story.

They are decided by a single concept.

Likelihood of confusion.

This concept is often misunderstood.

It does not require two names to be identical. It does not require direct copying. It does not even require proof that confusion has already occurred.

It asks a different question.

Would customers believe that the two brands come from the same source?

This shifts the entire analysis.

Because the focus is no longer on ownership alone.

It is on perception.

Two names can be different on paper and still create confusion in the market.

They may look similar at a glance. They may sound alike when spoken. They may suggest the same idea or impression.

In isolation, those similarities may appear minor.

In context, they may be enough.

The relationship between the businesses also matters.

If both operate in the same industry, the risk increases. If they operate in related markets, the risk may still exist. If the products or services are offered through the same channels, the likelihood of overlap grows.

The closer the connection, the greater the potential for confusion.

Strength plays a role as well.

Not all trademarks carry the same weight.

A strong, distinctive brand receives broader protection. It occupies more space in the market. It is easier to enforce because it is clearly defined.

A weak or descriptive brand receives less protection. Its boundaries are narrower. Competitors can move closer without crossing a clear line.

This difference often determines the outcome before the case even begins.

Evidence can reinforce the position.

Actual confusion, customers contacting the wrong company, making mistaken purchases, or expressing uncertainty, can strengthen a claim. But it is not required.

The absence of evidence does not mean the absence of risk.

It simply means the analysis must rely more heavily on the likelihood itself.

Intent is sometimes considered, but it is not decisive.

If the other party intentionally copied the brand, it may strengthen the case. But even without intent, infringement can exist.

Trademark law does not require bad behavior.

It requires confusing behavior.

There are also assumptions that often lead businesses in the wrong direction.

Registration alone does not guarantee success. It establishes rights, but those rights must still be evaluated within the context of the market.

Being larger does not create an advantage. Size does not determine confusion.

Operating in different categories does not eliminate risk if those categories are related in the eyes of the customer.

These are not technical distinctions.

They are practical ones.

This is why many cases fail.

Not because the brand lacks value.

But because the claim does not align with how the market perceives the situation.

A company may feel that its position is clear. It may believe the other party has crossed a line. But if that line is not visible to the customer, the argument weakens.

And in trademark law, the customer's perspective is the one that matters.

Before moving toward litigation, strategic companies pause.

They evaluate the strength of their mark. They assess the similarity of the names. They consider the overlap between the businesses. They look for evidence that supports the claim.

They also consider alternatives.

Not every situation requires a lawsuit. Some can be resolved through communication. Others through coexistence. In some cases, the cost of enforcement outweighs the benefit.

The objective is not to win every dispute.

It is to act where the position is strongest.

There is a principle in strategy that applies directly here.

The battle is not fought on paper.

It is fought in perception.

Companies that understand this build their brands differently.

They choose stronger names. They maintain consistency. They define their position clearly.

So, when a conflict arises, the advantage already exists.

Not because of what they argue.

But because of how they are seen.

Most businesses think:

"They copied us, we'll win."

Strategic operators ask a different question.

Will the market be confused?

Closing Observation

They focused on what was taken.
The decision turned on what customers saw.

Chapter 19

Brand Consistency: The Hidden Factor That Makes or Breaks Trademark Rights

Most companies believe branding is about creativity.

They change logos. They adjust messaging. They experiment with new visuals. They update their identity to reflect growth, trends, or internal preferences.

From the outside, it looks like progress.

From a trademark perspective, it can quietly weaken everything.

Strategic Principle

> *"In the midst of chaos, there is also opportunity."* Sun Tzu

Order creates strength. Chaos creates vulnerability.

A trademark works because it is recognized.

That recognition does not come from a single interaction. It is built over time, through repetition, through consistency, and through stability.

When a customer sees the same name, the same presentation, and the same experience repeatedly, something forms.

Memory.

And memory is what gives a trademark its power.

When that consistency breaks, the effect is subtle.

The brand begins to appear in slightly different ways. The name varies. The design shifts. The messaging changes depending on the platform or the product.

None of these changes appear significant on their own.

But over time, they accumulate.

And as they do, recognition weakens.

This is where most companies misunderstand the role of branding.

They believe variation creates freshness.

In reality, variation often creates confusion.

And confusion weakens position.

From a legal perspective, consistency is not optional.

Trademark rights are built on use in commerce.

But not just any use.

Consistent use.

If a brand appears in multiple forms, it becomes harder to define what the trademark actually is. The boundaries blur. The identity becomes less clear.

And when the identity is less clear, enforcement becomes more difficult.

This is why inconsistency creates risk.

Not because it looks unprofessional.

But because it weakens the foundation of the trademark itself.

Jobs Today: What He Controlled (And Why It Mattered)

Steve Jobs did not allow Apple to evolve through variation.

He enforced consistency.

The name appeared the same. The visual identity remained controlled. The experience across products, packaging, and environments aligned with a single standard.

This was not about design preference.

It was about control.

Customers did not have to interpret what Apple was. They recognized it at once. The brand did not shift depending on context.

It stayed stable.

Because of that stability, the trademark carried weight. It was clear. It was defined. It was enforceable.

Jobs did not build recognition through change.

He built it through repetition.

The contrast is clear.

A brand that is consistent becomes stronger over time.

A brand that changes constantly becomes fragmented.

The most common form of inconsistency appears in the name itself.

Companies begin to use variations. Slight adjustments. More words. Different formats depending on context.

Each variation feels harmless.

But over time, the question emerges.

What is the trademark?

If the answer is unclear, the position weakens.

Visual inconsistency follows a similar pattern.

Logos are updated frequently. Colors shift. Design elements change across platforms. What appears on a product differs from what appears online.

The customer begins to see multiple versions of the same brand.

Recognition becomes less immediate.

Messaging introduces another layer.

If the brand communicates different values in different places, performance in one context, affordability in another, luxury in a third, it becomes difficult to define what it stands for.

And if the brand cannot be defined, it cannot be defended.

The problem becomes more pronounced as the business grows.

More products are introduced. More partners become involved. More channels are added.

Each layer increases the risk of inconsistency.

Without control, the brand fragments.

This fragmentation affects more than perception.

It affects legal strength.

A company trying to enforce a trademark must show that the mark is used consistently. That the trademark represents a specific source. That customers associate it with a defined identity.

If multiple versions exist, that argument becomes more difficult.

The trademark begins to look less like a single asset and more like a collection of variations.

Consistency also affects value.

A brand that is stable can scale. It can expand into new markets. It can be licensed. It can be transferred.

A brand that is inconsistent struggles to do all of those things.

Because it lacks a clear identity to carry forward.

There is a principle in strategy that applies directly here.

Control the message, and you control the outcome.

If a company controls how its brand appears, it controls how it is perceived. If it allows variation, it allows the market to interpret the brand in different ways.

And once interpretation replaces control, position weakens.

Most companies believe they need to evolve their brand.

Strategic companies understand something more precise.

They need to protect recognition.

Closing Observation

They kept improving the brand.
They stopped repeating it.

Chapter 20

From Idea to Brand: The System Most Businesses Never Build

Every business begins in the same place.

An idea.

A product.
A service.
An opportunity that appears worth pursuing.

At that stage, the focus is always the same.

Build quickly.
Launch.
Adjust as the market responds.

From an operational perspective, that approach can work.

From a brand perspective, it creates risk.

Strategic Principle

> *"Victorious warriors win first, then go to war."* Sun Tzu

The strongest position is built before the market ever sees you.

Most businesses do not fail because of their product.

They failed because the structure around the product was never designed.

The name is chosen quickly. The search is rushed or skipped. Filing is delayed. Use becomes inconsistent. Ownership is unclear. Expansion is reactive.

Individually, each decision appears manageable.

Together, they create a system that lacks control.

A brand is not discovered.

It is built.

And building it correctly requires more than a sequence of actions.

It requires a system.

That system begins with the name.

Not as a creative decision, but as a strategic one. The name determines how easily the brand can be protected, how clearly it can be defined, and how far it can expand.

A weak name creates limitations that appear later. A strong name creates space.

Everything that follows depends on that foundation.

Once the name is selected, the next step is not filing.

It is understanding risk.

Before a business commits to a brand, it must understand the landscape in which that brand will exist. Similar names, related industries, existing uses: these define the boundaries.

Without that understanding, the business is building on uncertainty.

Filing comes next.

And timing is what determines position.

A company that files early secures its place before the market becomes crowded. A company that waits risks losing priority, regardless of how long the idea existed.

At this stage, the brand is not yet visible.

But the position is already forming.

Protection must then align with how the business operates.

Not just what it sells, but how it sells it. The categories in which the trademark is filed should reflect the structure of the business: products, services, channels, and anticipated growth.

Overextending creates unnecessary cost. Under-protecting creates gaps.

Alignment is what creates strength.

From the moment the brand enters the market, consistency becomes critical.

The name must appear the same way. The presentation must remain stable. The experience must align with what the brand represents.

This is not about aesthetics.

It is about recognition.

And recognition is what gives a trademark its value.

Ownership must also be defined early.

The question is not who uses the brand.

It is who controls it.

If ownership is unclear, control is unclear. If control is unclear, the business becomes difficult to manage, expand, or evaluate.

Structure determines outcome.

As the business grows, distribution becomes the next point of leverage.

Who is allowed to sell the product. Where it appears. How it is presented.

These decisions shape pricing, perception, and long-term positioning.

Without control, expansion introduces inconsistency.

With control, expansion reinforces strength.

Growth also introduces opportunity.

Licensing, partnerships, new markets.

But these opportunities only work if the system can support them.

A brand that is not clearly defined, consistently used, and properly structured cannot be extended without weakening.

Expansion, without control, creates instability.

Enforcement completes the system.

Not as a reaction, but as a decision.

Not every conflict requires action. But some do. And when action is taken, it must be timed correctly, supported by a strong position, and aligned with the overall strategy.

The objective is not to fight often.

It is to win when it matters.

There is a final perspective that most businesses overlook.

Value.

Even if a company never intends to sell, it is constantly being evaluated, by partners, by investors, by the market itself.

A brand that is clear, controlled, and consistent carries forward. It supports growth. It reduces risk. It creates leverage.

A brand that lacks structure does the opposite.

What becomes clear, when viewed as a whole, is that none of these elements operate independently.

The name affects protection.
Protection affects enforcement.
Enforcement affects perception.
Perception affects value.

Each decision connects to the next.

And over time, those connections define the position of the business.

Most founders approach branding as a series of steps.

Choose a name. File a trademark. Launch a product. Address issues as they arise.

Strategic operators approach it differently.

They build a system.

One that aligns the name, the structure, the protection, the use, and the expansion of the brand from the beginning.

Not perfectly.

But intentionally.

Because once the brand enters the market, the conditions begin to change.

Competitors appear. Channels expand. Opportunities emerge.

And at that point, the advantage belongs to the company that prepared for it.

Closing Observation

They built the business as they went.
The system was never built with it.

Part IV: Advanced Control & Market Dominance

Chapter 21

Trademark Due Diligence: What Buyers Look for Before Acquiring Your Brand

Most business owners believe a transaction is driven by numbers.

Revenue.
Profit.
Growth.

And in the initial stages of a deal, that is true.

But as the process moves forward, something changes.

The focus shifts.

Not to what has been built.

But to what can be trusted.

Strategic Principle

"The general who wins makes many calculations before the battle is fought." Sun Tzu

Serious buyers do not assume strength. They verify it.

Due diligence is not a formality.

It is a test.

A buyer is not simply reviewing the business. They are analyzing whether the asset they are acquiring can be controlled, transferred, and protected after the transaction is complete.

And that analysis converges in one place.

The trademark.

When a buyer acquires a company, they are not purchasing operations alone.

They are purchasing the right to control the brand going forward.

If that right is unclear, the deal does not collapse immediately.

It slows.

Then it adjusts.

And in some cases, it disappears entirely.

The first issue is always ownership.

Not assumed ownership.

Documented ownership.

Who holds the trademark?
Is it the operating company?
Is it a separate entity?
Has it been properly assigned?

These are not technical questions.

They are control questions.

If ownership is unclear, the buyer cannot be certain that the brand will transfer cleanly.

And uncertainty is where value begins to erode.

From there, the analysis becomes more precise.

The buyer examines the chain of title.

Not just who owns the mark today, but how it arrived there.

Every assignment. Every transfer. Every document that connects the original filing to the current owner.

If that chain is incomplete, the entire asset becomes vulnerable.

Because ownership is only as strong as its documentation.

Scope is next.

What does the trademark cover?

Not in theory.

In practice.

Does it align with the business?
Does it cover the products and services generating revenue?
Does it extend to the markets where the company operates, or intends to operate?

A mismatch here creates exposure.

And exposure creates negotiation leverage for the buyer.

Strength becomes unavoidable at this stage.

Not all trademarks are equal.

A distinctive name creates distance from competitors. It is easier to enforce. It occupies more space in the market.

A descriptive or weak name does the opposite.

It narrows protection. It invites proximity. It limits control.

This difference does not appear gradually in a deal.

It appears immediately.

Use is then examined.

Not whether the trademark has been used.

But how it has been used.

Is it consistent?
Is it aligned across products, platforms, and materials?
Does it clearly represent an only source?

If the brand appears in multiple forms, the buyer sees fragmentation.

And fragmentation introduces doubt.

Consistency reinforces this analysis.

A brand that is stable is easier to evaluate.

A brand that varies creates questions.

Which version is protected?
Which version matters?
Which version is being acquired?

If those questions cannot be answered clearly, the asset weakens.

Risk is then layered into the evaluation.

Existing conflicts.
Pending disputes.
Similar marks in the market.

The buyer is not only acquiring the brand.

They are acquiring its problems.

And if those problems are unclear, they are priced conservatively.

Enforcement history follows.

Has the company protected its brand?

Or has it tolerated infringement?

A lack of enforcement does not go unnoticed.

It signals that the boundaries of the brand may not be as strong as they appear.

And if the company has not protected it, the buyer begins to question whether it can be protected going forward.

Third-party use introduces another dimension.

Licenses.
Distribution agreements.
Partner relationships.

If others are using the brand, under what terms?

Are those terms controlled?

Or are they open, inconsistent, and difficult to manage?

Because what the buyer acquires is not just the brand.

It is every agreement attached to it.

International coverage becomes relevant for businesses that operate beyond a single market.

Where is the trademark protected?

Where is it not?

Are key markets exposed?

Because expansion depends on protection.

And without it, growth becomes limited.

Arnault's Standard: Why Certainty Commands a Premium

Bernard Arnault does not acquire brands based on potential alone.

He acquires control.

The brands within his portfolio are not only recognized, but they are also structured. Ownership is clear. Use is consistent. Distribution is controlled. The position is defined.

There is no ambiguity.

And because there is no ambiguity, value increases.

Not because the products are different.

But because the asset is certain.

This is the distinction that defines outcomes in transactions.

Buyers do not walk away from growth.

They walk away from uncertainty.

Most companies approach due diligence as a phase.

Something that happens during the deal.

Something to be addressed when necessary.

Strategic companies approach it differently.

They prepare before the deal exists.

They align ownership.
They organize records.
They ensure consistency.
They identify and resolve risks early.

So that when the review begins, there is nothing to explain.

Only something to confirm.

There is a principle in strategy that applies directly here.

Remove doubts before negotiation.

Because once doubt enters the conversation, it does not leave.

It is priced.

In the end, a buyer is not paying for what the business claims.

They are paying for what the business can prove.

And at that moment, the trademark is no longer a legal detail.

It is the decision point.

Closing Observation

The business told a strong story.
The brand determined whether it was believable.

Chapter 22

Vertical Distribution: How Smart Brands Control the Entire Market

Most businesses believe distribution is about reach.

The objective seems obvious.

Get the product in as many places as possible. Increase exposure. Expand availability. Let the market decide.

First, this approach creates growth.

More sellers.
More channels.
More visibility.

But over time, something begins to happen.

Prices start to move.
Presentation becomes inconsistent.
The brand appears differently depending on where it is encountered.

What looked like expansion begins to feel like loss of control.

Strategic Principle

> *"He who controls the supply routes controls the outcome of the war."* Sun Tzu

Control how your product reaches the market, and you control everything that follows.

Two companies can sell the same product.

They can offer similar quality, similar pricing, and similar positioning.

Yet one dominates.

The difference is rarely the product.

It is the system that surrounds it.

And at the center of that system is distribution.

Most businesses participate in distribution.

Strategic companies design it.

Busch Today: What He Built (And What Still Works)

Adolphus Busch did not rely on selling beer alone.

He built control around it.

At a time when most producers depended on independent distributors and inconsistent supply chains, Busch made a different decision. He invested in how his product moved. He controlled transportation. He influenced where it was sold. He shaped how it appeared in the market.

He understood something that most businesses still miss.

The product does not determine control.

The path the product takes does.

If Busch were operating today, the tools would be different, but the strategy would be identical.

He would not ask how many sellers could carry his brand.

He would ask who should be allowed to.

He would define access.
He would structure relationships.
He would align incentives so that every participant in the system reinforced the brand rather than competing against it.

He would not attempt to control every transaction.

He would control the environment in which transactions occur.

This is where most businesses lose their position.

They confuse availability with strength.

They believe that more channels create more power.

Uncontrolled distribution creates internal competition.

Sellers begin to compete against each other rather than against the market. Price becomes the easiest variable to adjust. And once pricing begins to move, it rarely stabilizes on its own.

The brand, which once carried value, begins to erode.

Not because the product changed.

But because the system did.

Controlled distribution produces a different outcome.

Access is limited.
Participation is defined.
Expectations are clear.

Fewer sellers operate within the system, but they operate under aligned conditions.

Pricing stabilizes not because it is forced, but because the structure discourages instability.

Presentation remains consistent because it is required.

The brand carries the same meaning regardless of where it is encountered.

There are multiple ways this control appears.

Some companies limit distribution to selected partners: those who meet defined standards. Others assign territories, reducing direct competition between sellers. Some maintain a direct relationship with customers, controlling the entire experience from beginning to end.

Many combine these approaches.

The structure itself is not the point.

The intention behind it is.

The connection to trademarks is direct.

A company cannot control distribution without controlling its brand.

The trademark provides the leverage.

It defines who is allowed to use the name, how it must appear, and under what conditions it can be presented to the market.

Without that control, distribution becomes difficult to manage.

With it, the company gains influence over every level of the system.

This is why platforms like Amazon create tension.

They encourage open access. Multiple sellers. Immediate competition.

Without structure, this leads to price pressure and brand inconsistency.

The solution is not to avoid the platform.

It is to control how the brand exists within it.

Supply can be managed. Access can be limited. Enforcement can be applied where necessary.

The platform does not remove control.

It tests whether control exists.

There is also a strategic advantage that is often overlooked.

Controlled distribution reduces conflict.

When access is defined, fewer parties operate within the system. When fewer parties operate, fewer disputes arise. The company spends less time reacting and more time directing.

This is where the Art of War principle becomes clear.

Limit the battlefield, and you limit the number of battles.

Most businesses approach distribution by asking:

"How do we sell more?"

Strategic companies ask a different question.

"How do we control how selling happens?"

Because once that control is established, everything else follows.

Pricing stabilizes.
Brand perception strengthens.
Expansion becomes intentional rather than reactive.

And competitors are forced to respond within a system they did not design.

Closing Observation

They increased access to grow faster.
They lost control of how the market behaved.

Chapter 23

Using Multiple Entities to Control Risk, Taxes, and Brand Value

Most businesses begin with a single company.

Everything is placed inside it.

Operations.
Revenue.
Contracts.
Employees.
And the brand.

At the early stages, this feels efficient.

Simple to manage. Easy to understand. Direct.

And for a time, it works.

Strategic Principle

"The skillful general ensures his army is not defeated before seeking victory." Sun Tzu

Before you grow, you structure the business so it cannot be easily damaged.

The problem is not that a single-entity structure fails immediately.

The problem is that it exposes everything at once.

Because not all assets within a business are the same.

Some carry risk.

Others carry value.

And when both exist in the same place, risk and value become tied together.

An operating company is designed to function.

It enters into agreements. It hires employees. It interacts with customers. It assumes obligations. It carries liability as a natural consequence of activity.

Exposure is part of its role.

A brand is different.

It does not engage in daily operations. It does not conduct transactions. What it holds is recognition, positioning, and the ability to generate future value.

It is the asset that drives the business forward.

When both are placed in the same entity, the most valuable asset becomes exposed to the highest level of risk.

And that exposure is rarely intentional.

The alternative is not complexity for its own sake.

It is structure with purpose.

Strategic companies separate functions across entities.

One entity operates the business.

Another holds the brand.

The operating company continues to do what it is designed to do.

It sells products. It manages operations. It carries risk.

The entity holding the trademark does something different.

It controls the asset.

The relationship between the two is defined, not assumed.

The operating company does not simply use the brand.

It is granted the right to use it.

Under terms.

Under conditions.

Under control.

This is where leverage begins.

Because the entity that owns the trademark controls how the brand is used.

It determines how expansion occurs.

It defines how others can participate in the system.

And most importantly, it exists outside the direct exposure of daily operations.

This separation creates several effects.

First, it isolates risk.

If the operating company faces a dispute, a liability event, or financial pressure, the brand is not automatically pulled into that exposure.

The business may face difficulty.

The asset remains intact.

Second, it defines control.

Ownership determines authority.

The entity holding the trademark sets the terms under which the business operates around it.

Not through daily management.

But through structure.

Third, it creates flexibility.

A brand held separately can be licensed, expanded, or leveraged across multiple entities. New ventures can be created. New markets can be entered.

Without restructuring the entire business.

Because the asset is not tied to a single operation.

Fourth, it affects value.

When a business is evaluated, clarity of structure matters.

A brand that is cleanly owned, clearly licensed, and properly documented increases confidence.

A brand that is embedded within an exposed structure introduces questions.

And questions reduce value.

There is often a misconception that multiple entities are created for tax reasons.

That is not the starting point.

Tax outcomes depend on jurisdiction, compliance, and proper planning.

Structure should first be designed for control and protection.

Efficiency follows when the structure is implemented correctly.

The mistake most businesses make is waiting.

They assume structure can be addressed later.

After growth.

After expansion.

After the business becomes more complex.

But restructuring is rarely simple.

Ownership becomes layered. Agreements must be revised. Tax implications arise. What could have been designed early becomes difficult to correct.

And by that stage, the cost of fixing the structure often exceeds the cost of building it correctly from the beginning.

There is also a risk in creating structure without substance.

Entities that exist only on paper, without real agreements or real activity, do not provide protection.

They create the appearance of control.

But not the reality.

A structure only works if it is real.

If ownership is documented.
If relationships are defined.
If agreements are enforceable.

Without those elements, separation does not hold.

There is a principle that applies across strategy.

Control the flow, and you control the outcome.

In business, flow appears in multiple forms.

Revenue.
Risk.
Ownership.

And structure determines how those elements move.

Most businesses think in terms of simplicity.

One company. One structure. One system.

Strategic companies think in terms of control.

They design where risk lives.

They decide where value is held.

And they ensure that the two are not unnecessarily exposed to each other.

Because once growth begins, structure is no longer theoretical.

It becomes the framework that determines what can be protected, what can be expanded, and what can be transferred.

Closing Observation

They built everything in one place.
They did not separate what needed protection from what created risk.

Chapter 24

Trademark Licensing vs. Franchising: Structuring Deals the Right Way

Most business owners believe licensing and franchising are variations of the same idea.

Someone uses the brand.
Someone pays a fee.
The business expands.

At a surface level, the structures appear similar.

But beneath that surface, they operate on entirely different ground.

And misunderstanding that difference does not create a small problem.

It creates exposure.

Strategic Principle

> *"He who knows the terrain will not be imperiled."* Sun Tzu

What looks similar can carry completely different consequences.

Licensing is centered on the brand.

A company allows another party to use its trademark under defined conditions. The licensee operates its own business. It makes its own decisions. It assumes its own operational responsibility.

The licensor controls something more precise.

How the brand is used.

Franchising goes further.

It is not limited to the brand.

It extends into the business itself.

The franchisor does not only control how the trademark appears. It controls how the business operates. It defines systems, processes, and methods. It creates a structure that can be replicated across locations with consistency.

The brand and the business become inseparable.

At first, the difference may appear conceptual.

In practice, it is structural.

The law does not rely on labels.

It does not ask what the parties intended to create.

It evaluates what the relationship actually is.

And in that evaluation, three elements become central.

The use of a trademark.
The payment of a fee.
And a level of control or assistance that extends into how the business operates.

When those elements exist together, the classification may shift.

Regardless of what the agreement is called.

This is where most problems begin.

Not through deliberate design.

But through gradual expansion.

A company starts with a license.

It allows another party to use the brand. It defines how the trademark must appear. It establishes quality standards.

Everything remains within the expected structure.

Then control increases.

Guidance is added. Processes are suggested. Systems are introduced to improve consistency.

Each addition feels reasonable.

Each addition appears to strengthen the brand.

Over time, the distinction begins to blur.

Guidance becomes expectation.

Expectation becomes requirement.

And the relationship begins to resemble something else.

At that point, the structure may no longer function as a license.

It may be treated as a franchise.

This shift carries consequences.

Franchising is regulated.

It requires disclosures. It imposes compliance obligations. It introduces timelines, documentation requirements, and oversight that do not exist in the same way within licensing structures.

What was intended as a flexible growth model becomes a regulated system.

Not because the strategy was wrong.

But because the structure was not controlled.

The critical distinction lies in control.

In a licensing relationship, the company controls the brand.

It defines how the trademark is used, how it is presented, and how its identity is preserved.

It does not control how the business is run.

In a franchising relationship, the company controls both.

The brand.

And the system.

This is where discipline becomes necessary.

Because control, when applied correctly, protects the brand.

When applied too broadly, it changes the structure.

There are forms of control that move a relationship toward franchising.

Requirements that dictate how services must be delivered. Systems that define daily operations. Mandatory training programs that shape how the business functions. Restrictions that extend beyond brand presentation into business processes.

Each of these may appear to improve consistency.

But together, they begin to define the business itself.

The objective is not to avoid control.

It is to apply it precisely.

A well-structured licensing agreement focuses on what must be protected.

The use of the trademark.
The quality associated with it.
The consistency of its presentation.

It defines these elements clearly.

But it does not extend into how the licensee runs its operations.

That boundary preserves the structure.

Franchising, when chosen intentionally, can be powerful.

It allows for replication of a complete business model. It creates uniform customer experiences. It enables rapid expansion across multiple locations.

But it requires preparation.

It requires compliance.

And it requires a willingness to operate within a regulated framework.

The mistake is not choosing one over the other.

The mistake is moving from one to the other without realizing it.

There is a principle in strategy that applies directly here.

Control must be aligned with intent.

If the goal is to license the brand, control must remain focused on the brand.

If the goal is to replicate the business, then the structure must be built as a franchise from the beginning.

Most businesses approach growth by asking:

"How can we expand faster?"

Strategic businesses ask a more precise question.

"What structure are we actually creating?"

Because once the structure is in place, it determines everything that follows.

The level of control.
The level of risk.
The obligations that arise.

And the flexibility that remains.

Closing Observation

They thought they were licensing the brand.
They had already begun building a system.

Chapter 25

How to Build a Brand That Investors Actually Want to Fund

Most founders believe investors fund ideas.

A strong concept.
A promising product.
A market with potential.

At the earliest stages, which may be enough to begin a conversation.

But as capital becomes serious, the criteria change.

Investors are not funding ideas.

They are funding outcomes they can predict.

Strategic Principle

"The general who wins makes many calculations before the battle is fought."
Sun Tzu

Translation:
Capital follows companies that have already removed uncertainty.

Every investor sees risk.

The question is not whether risk exists.

It is how much of it remains.

A business with an unclear brand, weak protection, inconsistent use, and uncontrolled distribution introduces uncertainty at every level.

A business with a structured, protected, and controlled brand reduces that uncertainty.

And when uncertainty is reduced, capital becomes easier to deploy.

This is where most founders misjudge the role of the brand.

They treat it as a marketing function.

A logo. A message. A way to present the business.

Investors do not evaluate branding at that level.

They evaluate the brand as a system.

A system that determines whether the company can defend its position, scale its operations, and maintain control as it grows.

Jobs Today: What Investors See (Before the Numbers)

When Steve Jobs rebuilt Apple, he did not begin with complexity.

He began with clarity.

The brand stood for something precise. It was consistent. It was controlled. It was aligned across every product and every interaction.

From an investor's perspective, that clarity mattered more than any individual feature.

Because clarity creates predictability.

A brand that is clearly defined is easier to scale. It is easier to extend into new products. It is easier to communicate in the market.

It reduces uncertainty before growth even begins.

Jobs did not build a company that needed to be explained.

He built one that could be understood immediately.

And that is what capital responds to.

Investors look for defensibility.

Not in theory.

In practice.

Can the company prevent competitors from moving into the same space? Can the brand be protected? Does it create distance, or does it invite comparison?

If the brand can be replicated easily, the investment carries risk.

If the brand creates barriers, the investment gains strength.

Clarity follows.

What does the brand represent?

Who is it for?

Why does it matter?

If those answers are not immediately visible, growth becomes unpredictable.

And unpredictability is something investors avoid.

Trademark protection becomes central at this stage.

Not as a legal formality.

As a sign of control.

Is the trademark registered? Is it strong? Is it enforceable? Are there conflicts? Are there risks that could surface later?

A missing or weak trademark is not a minor issue.

It is a structural weakness.

Because without protection, there is no control.

Scalability is evaluated next.

Can the brand extend beyond its current position?

Into new products. New markets. New channels.

A descriptive or narrow brand limits expansion. A strong, distinctive brand creates flexibility.

Investors are not funding what exists today.

They are funding what can exist tomorrow.

Consistency reinforces everything.

A brand that appears the same across products, platforms, and markets signals discipline. It signals control. It signals that the company understands its position.

A brand that varies introduces doubt.

And doubt reduces confidence.

Distribution plays a role that is often overlooked.

Who sells the product? How is it presented? Can competitors enter easily? Does pricing remain stable, or is it driven by uncontrolled competition?

If distribution is open, growth becomes unpredictable.

If distribution is controlled, growth becomes structured.

And structure attracts capital.

There is a pattern that emerges.

Strong brands reduce questions.

Weak brands create them.

And in a funding environment, every unanswered question becomes a point of hesitation.

The impact on valuation is direct.

A company with a strong brand commands higher multiples. It negotiates from a position of strength. It attracts better capital.

A company with a weak or unclear brand faces scrutiny. It encounters resistance. It accepts adjustments that reduce value.

Not because the product is different.

But because the risk is.

There is a principle that applies across every investment decision.

Capital does not chase potential alone.

It moves toward certainty.

Most founders think:

"We will build the product, then raise capital."

Strategic founders think differently.

They build something that can be funded.

Because the question is not whether the business can grow.

It is whether that growth can be controlled.

And that answer is built into the brand long before the investor ever sees it.

Closing Observation

The idea created interest.
The brand determined whether capital followed.

Chapter 26

The Real Value of a Trademark: How to Calculate Brand Worth

Most business owners believe their value comes from what they can see.

Revenue.
Inventory.
Operations.

These are measurable. They are immediate. They define the business.

But when companies are funded, acquired, or scaled, the valuation tells a different story.

A significant portion of the value is not tied to what the company does.

It is tied to what the company controls.

And that control lives in the brand.

Strategic Principle

"Opportunities multiply as they are seized." Sun Tzu

A strong position does not just hold value: it creates more of it.

There is no fixed price for a trademark.

No universal formula that produces a single number.

A brand is not valued by what it is.

It is valued by what it allows the business to do.

This distinction changes how value is understood.

A trademark does not sit on a balance sheet as a static asset.

It operates.

It influences pricing.
It shapes customer behavior.
It determines how far the business can expand.

And because of that, its value is dynamic.

The first place this value appears is in pricing.

Two products can be identical in cost, identical in function, and identical in distribution.

Yet one sells for more.

Not because it is different.

But because it is perceived differently.

A strong brand allows a company to charge more without losing demand. It reduces the need to compete on price. It protects margins even when competitors attempt to undercut.

That difference, the ability to hold price, is not accidental.

It is brand driven.

And over time, it compounds into measurable value.

The second layer is loyalty.

A recognizable trademark creates familiarity. Familiarity creates trust. And trust reduces friction in future transactions.

Customers return more easily. They require less convincing. The cost of acquiring them decreases over time.

Revenue becomes more predictable.

And predictability is one of the most valuable characteristics a business can have.

Because predictable revenue reduces perceived risk.

And reduced risk increases value.

The third layer is expansion.

A strong trademark is not limited to its original product.

It can extend.

Into new categories.
Into new markets.
Into new partnerships.

A business that sells one product today can grow into multiple offerings under the same brand. Licensing is possible. New channels become accessible.

The brand becomes a platform.

And platforms carry more value than isolated products.

At its core, value is not additive.

It is leverage.

A trademark creates leverage over customers, over competitors, and over partners. It shapes how the market interacts with the business.

The more leverage it creates, the more valuable it becomes.

There are established ways to measure this value.

None of them rely on guesswork.

They rely on performance.

One approach evaluates income.

It asks a direct question.

How much of the company's earnings are driven by the brand?

If a business generates significant revenue because of recognition, trust, and pricing power, a portion of that income can be attributed to the trademark.

Value follows that contribution.

Another approach examines royalties.

It asks a different question.

If the company did not own the brand, what would it have to pay to use it?

This creates a hypothetical licensing scenario.

A percentage of revenue is assigned as a royalty. That percentage reflects the value of the brand in practical terms.

If others would pay to use the trademark, then the trademark has measurable worth.

A third approach looks outward.

It compares similar transactions.

For what have comparable brands sold? What multiples were applied? What factors influenced those outcomes?

This method relies on context.

And when the context is clear, it reinforces valuation.

Despite these methods, many businesses misjudge their brand.

They either underestimate it, treating it as secondary to operations, or overestimate it without building the structure to support the claim.

In both cases, the issue is the same.

Value has not been aligned with reality.

Certain weaknesses reduce value immediately.

A name that is descriptive or generic limits protection. A lack of registration creates uncertainty. Inconsistent use weakens recognition. Open distribution erodes pricing control. A narrow structure limits expansion.

Each of these reduces leverage.

And when leverage decreases, value follows.

The opposite is also true.

Strong brands do not simply add value.

They multiply it.

They increase margins. They reduce risk. They attract better opportunities. They strengthen negotiation positions.

The impact is not linear.

It is exponential.

This is why the question most founders ask is the wrong one.

They ask:

"What is my brand worth?"

But value is not assigned after the fact.

It is built before the question is asked.

A stronger question is different.

Have you built something worth valuing?

Because a trademark becomes valuable through structure.

Through a distinctive name.
Through proper protection.
Through consistent use.
Through controlled distribution.
Through strategic expansion.
Through clear ownership.

Each of these elements contributes to the outcome.

There is a principle that applies across valuation.

The market does not reward effort.

It rewards control.

Most businesses believe value comes from revenue.

Strategic companies understand something more precise.

Value comes from what that revenue depends on.

And in many cases, what it depends on is not the product.

It is the brand that carries it.

Closing Observation

They looked at what the business earned.
They missed what made it possible.

Chapter 27

Trademark Strategy for E-Commerce Brands: Amazon, Shopify, and Beyond

From the outside, e-commerce appears simple.

A product is listed. Ads are run. Sales begin.

Growth feels immediate.

But beneath that surface, the structure is different.

The real battle is not about visibility.

It is about control.

Strategic Principle

"He who occupies the field of battle first and awaits his enemy is at ease." Sun Tzu

In digital markets, the company that establishes control first forces everyone else to react.

E-commerce is not a protected environment.

It is a copy market.

If a product succeeds, it will be replicated. Manufacturing is accessible. Competitors move quickly. Barriers to entry are low.

What appears unique at the beginning becomes common over time.

Products are temporary.

Brands are not.

This is where most businesses misjudge the landscape.

They believe they are building a product.

In reality, they are entering a system where anything without protection can be taken.

A trademark, in this environment, is not a formality.

It is the mechanism of control.

It determines who can use the name, who can present the product, and who can operate within the space the brand occupies.

Without it, enforcement becomes difficult.

And without enforcement, control disappears.

Nowhere is this more visible than on Amazon.

The platform is designed for access.

Multiple sellers can offer similar products. Listings can be shared. Pricing adjusts in real time based on competition.

From the platform's perspective, this increases efficiency.

From the brand's perspective, it creates risk.

A product that gains traction attracts attention.

Other sellers attach themselves to the listing. Variations appear. Counterfeits enter the system. Pricing begins to move.

What began as growth turns into competition within the same listing.

The brand no longer controls the experience.

It reacts to it.

This is why control of the listing becomes critical.

The listing is not just a page.

It is the point where perception, pricing, and conversion come together.

If control over that listing is lost, the company loses more than visibility.

It loses authority over the sale.

Trademark strategy is what allows that control to exist.

With proper registration, the company can access enforcement tools. It can remove infringing sellers. It can challenge unauthorized use. It can define how the brand appears.

Without that structure, the platform does not recognize ownership in the same way.

Visibility remains.

Control does not.

There are systems designed to support this control.

Amazon's Brand Registry is one of them.

It allows trademark owners to manage listings, remove infringers, and protect brand identity.

But the tool itself is not the advantage.

The advantage is the structure behind it.

Many sellers register for these programs and still fail to maintain control.

Because they approach the problem tactically rather than strategically.

They file weak trademarks. They fail to enforce consistently. They allow too many sellers into the system. They react instead of designing the environment.

The result is the same.

The brand becomes diluted.

Shopify presents a different structure.

It gives the company control over its own platform. The website, the presentation, and the customer experience are owned directly.

At first, this appears to solve the problem.

But it does not eliminate the need for protection.

The name must still be secured. The brand must still be controlled. Competitors can still operate in parallel markets.

Owning the platform does not replace owning the brand.

The core issue across all e-commerce channels is the same.

Access.

When access is unrestricted, competition increases. Sellers compete against each other. Price becomes the primary differentiator.

Margins compress.

And over time, the product becomes interchangeable.

Control changes that dynamic.

When access is defined, fewer participants operate within the system. Pricing stabilizes. Presentation remains consistent. The brand carries the same meaning regardless of where it appears.

The environment supports the business instead of working against it.

This is where most e-commerce strategies fail.

They focus on selling more.

They ignore controlling how selling happens.

The consequences are predictable.

Listings are hijacked.
Competitors enter easily.
Pricing declines.
Margins erode.

Not because the product failed.

But because the system was never controlled.

There is a principle that applies directly here.

Control the environment, and you control the outcome.

In e-commerce, that environment is digital.

Listings.
Platforms.
Search results.
Distribution channels.

Each of these can either reinforce the brand or weaken it.

The difference is whether the company has established control before growth begins.

Most sellers think:

"How do we increase sales?"

Strategic operators think differently.

"How do we control the system that produces those sales?"

Because in a market where everything can be copied, the only sustainable advantage is not the product.

It is the position.

Closing Observation

They focused on selling the product.
They never secured control over where it was sold.

Chapter 28

Common Trademark Mistakes That Cost Companies Millions

Most businesses do not fail because of bad products.

They fail because of decisions that seemed insignificant at the time.

A name chosen too quickly.
A filing delayed.
A risk ignored.

Individually, these decisions appear manageable.

Collectively, they define the outcome.

Strategic Principle

> *"If you are careless, your opponent will seize the advantage."* Sun Tzu

Loss of position rarely comes from a single mistake. It comes from small oversights that others take advantage of.

Trademark problems do not appear immediately.

They build.

Slowly.

A business launches with a name that feels clear but lacks strength. At first, there is no resistance. The market responds. Growth begins.

Only later does the limitation become visible.

Competitors move closer. Enforcement becomes difficult. The brand begins to blend into the category it was meant to define.

Other companies skip the search entirely or treat it as a formality.

A quick review. A surface-level check. Enough to feel comfortable moving forward.

The real conflicts remain hidden.

Months later, an application is refused. Or worse, a challenge appears after the brand has already gained traction.

At that point, the cost is no longer theoretical.

It is operational.

Rebranding, legal fees, and lost momentum begin to accumulate.

Not because the risk was unpredictable.

But because it was never fully evaluated.

Timing creates another pattern.

Filing is delayed.

Business launches first. The assumption is that protection can be addressed later.

But trademark law does not reward intention.

It rewards action.

Another party files. Priority shifts. And the company that built the brand is forced into a defensive position.

The position was available.

It was not secured.

Even when companies file, mistakes continue.

Applications are submitted without strategy. Categories are selected without alignment to the business. Descriptions are drafted without precision.

Protection appears to exist.

But gaps remain.

And those gaps become visible only when the brand is tested.

As the business grows, inconsistency begins to appear.

The name changes slightly across platforms. Logos evolve. Messaging shifts depending on context.

Each change feels minor.

But over time, the identity fragments.

Recognition weakens.

And when enforcement becomes necessary, the company struggles to define what it is protecting.

Distribution introduces another layer.

To grow, companies allow broad access.

Multiple sellers. Multiple channels. Limited restrictions.

At first, this increases reach.

Over time, it creates internal competition.

Prices begin to fall. Presentation varies. The brand loses its position.

Not because of external pressure.

But because control was never established.

Enforcement is often ignored.

Competitors move closer. Similar names appear. Infringing products enter the market.

The company notices.

But it does not act.

The assumption is that the impact is minimal.

Over time, tolerance becomes precedent.

And precedent weakens position.

Because what is not enforced becomes accepted.

Structure creates its own risks.

Ownership is unclear. The brand sits in the wrong entity. Agreements are missing or incomplete.

At first, nothing happens.

But when a transaction is considered, when investment is introduced or a sale is explored, the problem becomes visible.

Control cannot be confirmed.

And when control cannot be confirmed, value declines.

Expansion introduces the final layer.

The business grows beyond its original market.

But protection does not follow.

Other parties register the brand in new areas. Opportunities become blocked. Growth becomes restricted.

The company assumed expansion would be available.

It was not secured.

Each of these mistakes shares a common characteristic.

They are small at the beginning.

They do not create immediate consequences.

They feel manageable.

But over time, they compound.

Risk accumulates.
Control weakens.
Value erodes.

And by the time the impact becomes visible, the cost of correction is significant.

The real cost is not limited to money.

It appears in lost leverage.

A company that cannot enforce its brand negotiates from a weaker position. A company with unclear ownership struggles to close deals. A company with inconsistent use loses recognition.

Each of these reduces what the business can command.

There is a principle that applies across all these patterns.

Most problems are preventable.

Strong companies do not avoid mistakes by chance.

They avoid them by design.

They choose stronger names.
They evaluate risk before committing.
They file early.
They maintain consistency.
They control distribution.
They enforce when necessary.
They structure ownership clearly.
They plan for expansion.

These are not advanced strategies.

They are foundational decisions.

But they must be made early.

Because once the brand enters the market, correcting these issues becomes more difficult.

Most businesses operate with a simple mindset.

"We will fix problems when they arise."

Strategic businesses operate differently.

They prevent problems that can be avoided.

Because the difference between the two is not effort.

It is foresight.

Closing Observation

Nothing failed at the beginning.
The problems were already there.

Chapter 29

Exit Strategy: How to Structure Your Brand for Maximum Sale Value

Most business owners think about exit at the end.

When the company has grown.
When revenue has stabilized.
When a buyer appears.

At that point, attention shifts to valuation, negotiation, and deal terms.

But by then, the most important decisions have already been made.

The structure is set.
The ownership is defined.
The risks are embedded.

And the leverage is determined.

Strategic Principle

"Victorious warriors win first, then go to war." Sun Tzu

The strongest exits are built long before the deal begins.

Buyers do not pay for effort.

They pay for certainty.

Revenue may attract attention, but structure determines value. A company can generate strong income and still face a reduced valuation if the underlying framework introduces doubt.

And in most transactions, that doubt converges in one place.

The brand.

An exit-ready business is not defined by performance alone.

It is defined by clarity.

Who owns the trademark.
How that ownership is documented.
Whether it aligns with the structure of the business.

If ownership is unclear, the deal becomes unclear.

And uncertainty reduces value immediately.

This is why separation becomes powerful.

A brand that is held independently from operations creates flexibility. The operating company can be transferred. The brand can be retained. Licensing structures can be introduced.

The company is no longer limited to a single outcome.

It has options.

And in a transaction, options create leverage.

Protection reinforces this position.

A trademark that is properly registered, correctly scoped, and consistently used signals stability. It shows that the brand is not only valuable—but defensible.

A weak or unclear trademark introduces the opposite.

Risk.

And risk is always priced.

Consistency becomes visible at this stage.

A buyer is not evaluating how the brand looks in isolation.

They are evaluating whether it represents a single, stable identity.

If the brand appears differently across products, platforms, or markets, the question becomes unavoidable.

What exactly is being acquired?

If the answer is unclear, value declines.

Distribution also enters the analysis.

Who controls the market?

Are there too many sellers?
Is pricing stable?
Does the company define how the product reaches customers?

A controlled system signals strength.

An open system signals volatility.

And volatility reduces confidence.

Agreements must also be examined.

Licenses, distribution arrangements, partnerships: each must be clear, documented, and enforceable.

If relationships are informal, inconsistent, or poorly defined, they introduce risk.

And once again, risk affects price.

Because what is not documented cannot be relied upon.

Hidden issues create the greatest impact.

Pending disputes.
Unresolved conflicts.
Unclear rights in key markets.

These do not remain hidden during due diligence.

They surface.

And when they do, they shift the negotiation.

Not gradually.

Immediately.

There is a concept that defines the strongest exit positions.

Optionality.

A company that is structured correctly is not forced into a single path.

It can sell the entire business.
It can sell operations and retain the brand.
It can license the brand after the sale.
It can expand further before exiting.

Each option increases flexibility.

And flexibility strengthens negotiation.

The opposite is also true.

A company with a weak structure has fewer choices.

It must accept the terms available.

Because it cannot separate assets, cannot clarify ownership easily, and cannot remove risk without significant effort.

The negotiation becomes reactive.

This is where most businesses lose value.

Not because the business lacks potential.

But because the structure limits what can be done with it.

There is a consistent pattern across transactions.

Strong structures reduce questions.

Weak structures create them.

And every unanswered question becomes a point of leverage for the buyer.

The impact on valuation is direct.

A clear, controlled brand increases multiples. It reduces negotiation pressure. It attracts more serious buyers.

A weak or uncertain structure does the opposite.

It lowers value. It increases scrutiny. It slows the deal.

Not because the numbers changed.

But because the risk did.

Most business owners assume they will address these issues when the time comes.

When a buyer appears.
When the deal begins.

But by that stage, correction is difficult.

Ownership must be restructured. Agreements must be rewritten. Tax implications arise. Legal complexity increases.

What could have been designed early becomes expensive to fix.

There is a principle that applies across all strategic outcomes.

Preparation determines position.

The companies that achieve the strongest exits are not the ones that waited.

They are the ones that built with the exit in mind.

They aligned ownership.
They structured control.
They protected the brand.
They defined relationships.

So that when the opportunity appeared, nothing needed to be explained.

Only confirmed.

Most businesses think:

"We will figure it out when we sell."

Strategic companies think differently.

They build something that is ready to be sold.

Because in the end, the transaction is not decided in negotiation.

It is decided by the structure that exists before the conversation begins.

Closing Observation

They focused on the deal.
The outcome had already been set.

Chapter 30

Trademark Strategy Master Guide: How to Build, Protect, and Scale a Brand That Controls Its Market

Most businesses treat trademarks as paperwork.

A name is filed.

A registration is obtained.

And the process is considered complete.

From that point forward, the business moves on to what feels more immediate: sales, marketing, operations.

That approach creates something predictable.

Limited protection.

Weak positioning.

Unnecessary risk.

Because a trademark was never meant to be a task.

It was meant to be a system.

Strategic Principle

"All warfare is based on strategy." Sun Tzu

The outcome is not determined by isolated actions, but by the system that connects them.

A brand is not a name.

It is how the market sees the business.

A trademark is what allows that perception to be controlled.

Without that control, perception is shaped externally by competitors, by distributors, by the market itself.

With control, the business defines its position.

Everything in this book leads to a single realization.

A trademark strategy is not a legal checklist.

It is a business framework.

It begins at the foundation.

Before the product is launched, before the market is entered, the name must be chosen with intention. Not for clarity alone, but for control. A name that can be protected, enforced, and expanded.

From there, risk must be understood.

Not through surface-level checks, but through real analysis. The landscape must be evaluated before the brand is exposed. Because once exposure begins, position becomes harder to secure.

Filing follows.

Not as a formality, but as a decision that establishes priority. It defines who controls the name before the market can respond.

Protection then becomes structural.

The trademark must align with the business model, not only what is sold, but how it is sold. Ownership must be defined clearly. The entity that holds the brand must be positioned to protect it, separate from the risks of daily operations.

Consistency reinforces everything.

A brand that is used the same way, across all platforms and interactions, builds recognition. And recognition is what gives the trademark its strength.

Control emerges next.

Distribution must be defined. Not every seller should have access. Not every channel should operate without structure.

Because distribution determines pricing.

And pricing determines perception.

Enforcement becomes part of that control.

Not as constant action, but as selective action. The boundaries of the brand must be reinforced when necessary. Because what is tolerated becomes the standard.

Licensing, when applied correctly, allows the brand to expand without losing structure. But only when the system is clear enough to be repeated.

Scale introduces complexity.

Markets expand. Products evolve. Opportunities increase.

But expansion without protection creates exposure.

International strategy must be deliberate. Not every market requires immediate protection, but the right markets must be secured at the right time.

At this stage, the brand is no longer local.

It becomes a platform.

Value then becomes visible.

Not in abstract terms.

But in measurable effects.

Pricing power.

Customer loyalty.

Expansion potential.

Each of these contributes to how the business is evaluated.

And over time, the trademark becomes the asset that carries the company forward.

Preparation for exit completes the system.

Ownership must be clear.

Agreements must be defined.

Risks must be identified and resolved.

Because when a buyer appears, the structure is already in place.

The negotiation does not create value.

It reveals it.

When viewed as a whole, the system becomes clear.

It is not a sequence of independent decisions.

It is a connected structure.

The name affects protection.

Protection affects enforcement.

Enforcement affects perception.

Perception affects value.

And each element builds on the one before it.

Most businesses operate without this system.

They choose names quickly.

They file without strategy.

They expand without control.

They react to problems as they arise.

The result is predictable.

Weak protection.

Price competition.

Limited growth.

Lower valuation.

Strategic companies operate differently.

They design the system from the beginning.

They build with intention.

They protect with precision.

They control with discipline.

They scale with structure.

And because of that, they do not simply compete.

They define the market around them.

There is a final distinction that separates these two approaches.

Most businesses believe they need a trademark.

Strategic businesses understand something more important.

They need control.

Because in the end, a trademark is not just a legal right.

It is leverage.

It determines how the business is perceived.

How it is priced.

How it expands.

How it is valued.

And whether it leads or follows.

If you have reached this point, the difference is already clear.

The question is no longer whether trademarks matter.

The question is whether the system will be built correctly.

Closing Observation

They thought they needed a trademark.
They needed control over everything it touched.

EPILOGUE

There is a moment in every business when something shifts.

What began as an idea becomes real.
What felt experimental becomes valuable.
What seemed simple begins to carry weight.

At that moment, the question changes.

It is no longer:

"How do we grow?"

It becomes:

"How do we protect and control what we have built?"

Most companies arrive at that moment unprepared.

They have created something worth protecting.

But they have not built the structure to protect it.

That is why this book exists.

Not as a collection of concepts.

But as a system.

One that allows business owners to understand not only what they are building, but how to control it while it exists, and how to preserve its value when it is time to exit.

To my clients:

If this book is in your hands, it was not given to you by accident.

It was given to you so that you understand the asset you are building.

Not just the product.
Not just the revenue.

But the brand.

You are not simply creating something to sell.

You are creating something that can be controlled, expanded, and transferred.

And that only happens when the structure is built correctly.

To my daughter,
Juliet Alcoba:

This book is now part of your responsibility.

You will inherit not just a firm, but a philosophy.

One that goes beyond filing applications and responding to office actions.

Your role is to guide.

To ensure that the people who trust you understand what they are building.

To make sure they are not only protected—but positioned.

Give this book to every client.

Let it answer the questions they do not yet know how to ask.

Let it show them the value of what they are creating.

And more importantly, let it show them how to control it.

Because what we do is not transactional.

It is structural.

We are not simply securing rights.

We are helping build assets that define businesses, support families, and shape communities.

There will be moments when work feels routine.

Filings. Responses. Agreements.

But behind each of those actions is something larger.

A system taking form.

A position being secured.

A future being protected.

Carry that understanding forward.

Because the difference between a business that survives and a business that leads is not effort.

It is structure.

This book is only the beginning.

The real work happens in how it is applied.

Final Observation

They believed they were building a business.
They were building something far more valuable.

Continue the Strategy: Protect the Innovation

By now, the system should be clear.

A trademark allows you to control the market around your brand.

It defines how your business is seen, how it is positioned, and how it grows.

But there is another layer.

One that exists before the brand ever reaches the market.

The product itself.

A strong brand controls perception.

A strong patent controls competition.

If your business is built on innovation, something new, something functional, something that can be replicated—then control of the brand alone is not enough.

Because while the trademark defines who owns the name, the patent defines who owns the idea.

Without that protection, competitors can approach from a different angle.

They may not use your name.

But they can build around your product.

They can enter your space.

They can compete on function while you compete on identity.

This is where strategy must be complete.

The brand must be controlled.

And the innovation must be protected.

That is why this book was written as part of a broader framework.

In *Protect or Perish*, I address the other side of the equation.

Not how to control the market, but how to prevent others from entering it in the first place.

It is written for those who are building something that can be copied,

and who understand that speed alone is not a strategy.

If this book changed how you think about trademarks,

Protect or Perish will change how you think about innovation itself.

Continue the Strategy

Learn how to protect what you build at the product level:

Protect or Perish: The Complete Guide to Patent Strategy, Global Protection, and Avoiding Costly Mistakes

Available on Amazon and at: https://www.amazon.com/dp/B0GVZGCJDY

www.protectorperish.com

Final Connection

Control the brand.
Protect the product.

That is where real leverage begins.

About the Author

Ruben Alcoba is a Florida-based intellectual property attorney and the founder of Alcoba Law Group PA, a firm dedicated exclusively to patent and trademark prosecution.

With more than 25 years of experience and over 2,500 patents and trademark matters handled, he has represented entrepreneurs, startups, and established companies in securing, protecting, and scaling their most valuable business assets. He is trusted by founders, investors, and companies scaling into competitive markets to structure intellectual property as a strategic asset for control, growth, and long-term value.

Ruben focuses on what most businesses overlook: not just obtaining intellectual property rights but structuring them as systems that define how a business is positioned, how it expands, and how it is valued.

He holds a Master of Laws (LL.M.) in International Taxation and Financial Services from the Thomas Jefferson School of Law and earned his Juris Doctor from the University of Miami School of Law. His multidisciplinary background allows him to approach intellectual property not as an isolated legal function, but as part of a broader framework that includes business structure, taxation, and transaction strategy.

Ruben is also the author of:

Protect or Perish: The Complete Guide to Patent Strategy, Global Protection, and Avoiding Costly Mistakes

a strategic guide designed to help innovators protect their ideas before entering competitive markets.

Throughout his career, Ruben has collaborated with clients at every stage: from early-stage founders selecting and securing brand names, to growing companies expanding across markets and distribution channels, to established businesses preparing for investment, licensing, or exit.

This experience led to a clear realization: most companies do not lose value because of poor products. They lose value because they never built the structure to control what they created.

Control the Brand was written to address that gap. It reflects the same philosophy applied in his legal practice:

That a trademark is not simply a filing, it is a system that determines how a business is positioned, how it grows, and how it is valued.

Ruben advises clients on trademark strategy, brand protection, and intellectual property positioning from his office in Miami, Florida.

Connect

Website: www.miamipatents.com
Firm: www.alcobalaw.com
LinkedIn: https://www.linkedin.com/in/patent-attorney-ruben-alcoba/

If you are serious about building a brand that holds value:

Do not wait until there is a problem.

Structure it correctly from the beginning.

For trademark strategy, brand protection, and business structuring:

www.miamipatents.com

www.ingramcontent.com/pod-product-compliance
Lightning Source LLC
LaVergne TN
LVHW010947110826
845149LV00015B/3243

* 9 7 9 8 9 9 4 5 8 7 2 3 2 *